JESUS OF NAZARETH,

SOCIALIST OR CAPITALIST?

DAVID HOPE

ISBN 0-9772194-7-X

ISBN13 978-0-9772194-7-6

Library of Congress Control Number: 2011909832

Printed in the United States of America.

RevMedia Publishing
PO Box 5172
Kingwood, TX 77325

A publishing division of Revelation Ministries

www.revministries.com
www.revmedianetwork.com
www.revmediapublishing.com

TABLE OF CONTENTS

ACKNOWLEDGEMENTS

First of all, I would like to acknowledge my Lord and Savior, Jesus Christ, for making a way for all of us to choose eternal life and also prosper on earth. Without his wisdom, this book would not be possible.

To my wife Sandy, I thank you for being such a wonderful helpmeet. You are truly a Proverbs 31 woman. Your value is far above rubies!

To the people of Words of Life Church, I thank you for your encouragement and your continual support and belief in me.

To my publisher and friend David Yanez, I thank you for your encouragement and friendship.

To Gerald Davis, a special thanks for first exposing me to the Biblical concept of giving with receiving in mind over 23 years ago. Your teachings and friendship have been a blessing to me all these years.

Foreword

This book, *Jesus of Nazareth, Socialist or Capitalist*, needed to be written. Pastor David Hope has stepped out of the comfort zone into the combat zone to share truths that few in life would tackle. Jesus said the truth will set us free and the truths in this book will expose the lies of the enemy and produce liberty. It is critical in war to understand who the enemy is and how he operates.

As I've traveled all over the world, I've seen first hand the empty results of a socialist mindset. It promises prosperity for all at the expense of a select few who have worked hard to achieve their wealth and possessions. It puts its subjects into bondage and dependence upon the government.

Pastor David shares in this book that we as believers must avoid being passive toward Israel because she is God's chosen people and serves as a prophetic picture of the body of Christ. The enemy always attempts to change laws in an attempt to pull us out of knowing God's boundaries which He has given us through the Word. If we don't know these truths contained in this book it will be easy to enter into deception.

In 1966, I died and went to Heaven. Everyone there has their own mansion. There is no redistribution of wealth in Heaven, just rewards for the believer's faithfulness here on earth. The Bible teaches as it is in Heaven so it is here on earth. We are on earth to bring forth fruit for God's glory. It comes through our choice to obey God's ways over man's ways.

I admire Pastor David Hope for taking a stand on this subject. I thank God there are still prophetic voices like David's in the world today that are unashamed to boldly speak against a " politically correct" system to establish freedom to all who will hear God's message.

Dr. Gary L. Wood, THD
Evangelist & Apostle
Author of *A Place Called Heaven*

CHAPTER ONE

END-TIME HARVEST

During my lifetime, I have delivered food and the gospel to countless homeless people on the streets of Houston, Texas. After personal conversations with well over a hundred different homeless men, I have come to a conclusion. The vast majority of these men are homeless because they don't want anybody to tell them what to do--ever. They would rather not have a home than be accountable to someone else's authority.

This is a picture of the spiritual reality for those who will not find a home in heaven. People won't find a spiritual home in heaven for the same reason a natural man doesn't have a physical home on the earth. They refuse to submit to someone else's spiritual authority. They won't submit to Jesus and make Him Lord over their life.

"For God so loved the world, that he gave his only begotten Son, that whosoever believeth in him should not perish, but have everlasting life" (John 3:16).

Although everyone has the opportunity to have a home in heaven, because eternal life is a free gift of God offered to whosoever will receive it, not everyone will go to heaven when his or her natural body dies. Although eternal life is available to everyone, not everyone will want to submit to Jesus. Jesus confirms this in Mark chapter 16.

"And he said unto them, Go ye into all the world, and preach the gospel to every creature.
He that believeth and is baptized shall be saved; but he that believeth not shall be damned" (Mark 16:15-16).

Even though not everyone will be in heaven, a great many people *will* find a home there, especially in these last days. Have you ever heard of the great end-time harvest of souls? Is this a biblical principle, or did some preacher make this up?

Let's establish that the primary responsibilities of the Holy Spirit today, as he works through the church, are to build the church (including adding new converts) and to get the church ready, so that at the moment of Jesus' appearing, the church will be without spot, wrinkle or blemish.

"And I say also unto thee, that thou art Peter, and upon this rock I will build my church; and the gates of hell shall not prevail against it" (Matt. 16:18).

"That he might present it to himself a glorious church, not having spot, or wrinkle, or any such thing; but that it should be holy and without blemish" (Eph. 5:27).

Have you ever wondered why we don't immediately go to heaven when we are born again? If we didn't have a function as a member of the Body of Christ, it would be better for us to go directly to heaven after receiving Jesus as our savior. In heaven there is no more pain or sorrow. There is no more stress, no worries and no sickness. There is everlasting peace and joy.

Then why do we remain here on the earth to live out the rest of our lives? We remain so that we can fulfill our kingdom destiny. The

Lord wants to use us as we respond to his word and the leading of the Spirit to bring others to heaven with us. We also have unique gifts and talents to solve problems for others, to bless others, and help build up the body of Christ as we work in unity with our brothers and sisters in Christ. We are instruments of the Holy Spirit's work here on Earth.

"Now there are diversities of gifts, but the same Spirit. And there are differences of administrations, but the same Lord. And there are diversities of operations, but it is the same God which worketh all in all. But the manifestation of the Spirit is given to every man to profit withal" (1 Cor. 12:47).

When the church has done its job, Jesus will come for us.

"For the Lord himself shall descend from heaven with a shout, with the voice of the archangel, and with the trump of God: and the dead in Christ shall rise first: Then we which are alive and remain shall be caught up together with them in the clouds, to meet the Lord in the air: and so shall we ever be with the Lord. Wherefore comfort one another with these words" (1 Thess. 4:16-18).

Jesus will not come for a defeated, unsuccessful church. He will come for a church triumphant. Remember, Jesus is coming for a glorious church, one that has fulfilled its mission. You see, the church is not perfected through tribulation and trial, but through the God-given, Holy Spirit-anointed ministry of apostles, prophets, evangelists, pastors, and teachers.

"And he gave some, apostles; and some, prophets; and some, evangelists; and some, pastors and teachers; For the perfecting of the saints, for the work of the ministry, for the edifying of the body of Christ: Till we all come in the unity of the faith, and of the knowledge of the Son of God, unto a perfect man, unto the measure of the stature of the fulness of Christ: That we henceforth be no more children, tossed to and fro, and carried about with every wind of doctrine, by the sleight of men, and cunning craftiness, whereby they lie in wait to deceive; But speaking the truth in love, may grow up into him in all things, which is the head, even Christ" (Eph. 4:11-15).

We can see in Revelation chapter 4 (when the church is in heaven during the early part of the tribulation period), that the church triumphant is a vast multitude of people. The church did its job with excellence while it was still on the earth. The church is not comprised of a bunch of timid, milk-toast weaklings. We are more than conquerors through Christ Jesus! (See Romans 8:37).

Any oppression from Satan will only cause God's people to come out of Egypt (Egypt is always a biblical representation of the world), to quit blending in with the world, and become what God has called us to be. We are the head and not the tail, above only, not beneath, and the lender not the borrower.

"The LORD shall open unto thee his good treasure, the heaven to give the rain unto thy land in his season, and to bless all the work of thine hand: and thou shalt lend unto many nations, and thou shalt not borrow. And the LORD shall make thee the head, and not the tail; and thou shalt be above only, and thou shalt not be beneath; if that thou hearken unto the commandments of the LORD thy God, which I command thee this day, to observe and to do them" (Deut. 28:12-13).

Before the appearing of Jesus occurs, the church of Jesus Christ will become the strongest and most influential force on the face of the earth!

"I have given them thy word; and the world hath hated them, because they are not of the world, even as I am not of the world. I pray not that thou shouldest take them out of the world, but that thou shouldest keep them from the evil. They are not of the world, even as I am not of the world. Sanctify them through thy truth: thy word is truth. As thou hast sent me into the world, even so have I also sent them into the world. And for their sakes I sanctify myself, that they also might be sanctified through the truth. Neither pray I for these alone, but for them also which shall believe on me through their word; That they all may be one; as thou, Father, art in me, and I in thee, that they also may be one in us: that the world may believe that thou hast sent me. And the glory which thou gavest me I have given them; that they may be one, even as we are one: I in them, and thou in me, that they may be made perfect in one; and that the world may know that thou hast sent me, and hast loved them, as thou hast loved me. Father, I will that they also, whom thou hast given me, be with me where I am; that they may behold my glory, which thou hast given me: for thou lovedst me before the foundation of the world. O righteous Father, the world hath not known thee: but I have known thee, and these have known that thou hast sent me. And I have declared unto them thy name, and will declare it: that the love wherewith thou hast loved me may be in them, and I in them" (John 17:14-26).

"Now thanks be unto God, which always causeth us to triumph in Christ, and maketh manifest the savour of his knowledge by us in every place" (2 Cor. 2:14).

The mass of people in heaven representing the church is described to us in chapter 4 of the Book of Revelation.

"And immediately I was in the spirit: and, behold, a throne was set in heaven, and one sat on the throne. And he that sat was to look upon like a jasper and a sardine stone: and there was a rainbow round about the throne, in sight like unto an emerald. And round about the throne were four and twenty seats: and upon the seats I saw four and twenty elders sitting, clothed in white raiment; and they had on their heads crowns of gold. And out of the throne proceeded lightnings and thunderings and voices: and there were seven lamps of fire burning before the throne, which are the seven Spirits of God. And before the throne there was a sea of glass like unto crystal: and in the midst of the throne, and round about the throne, were four beasts full of eyes before and behind. And the first beast was like a lion, and the second beast like a calf, and the third beast had a face as a man, and the fourth beast was like a flying eagle. And the four beasts had each of them six wings about him; and they were full of eyes within: and they rest not day and night, saying, Holy, holy, holy, Lord God Almighty, which was, and is, and is to come. And when those beasts give glory and honour and thanks to him that sat on the throne, who liveth for ever and ever, The four and twenty elders fall down before him that sat on the throne, and worship him that liveth for ever and ever, and cast their crowns before the throne, saying, Thou art worthy, O Lord, to receive glory and honour and power: for thou hast created all things, and for thy pleasure they are and were created" (Rev. 4:2-11).

An elder is a person God chooses to represent him and minister to the saints. Jesus shares his ministry with those who are gifts to the body of Christ representing the church. They are people who feed the flock of God.[1]

"The elders which are among you I exhort, who am also an elder, and a witness of the sufferings of Christ, and also a partaker of the glory that shall be revealed: Feed the flock of God which is among you, taking the oversight thereof, not by constraint, but willingly;

not for filthy lucre, but of a ready mind; Neither as being lords over God's heritage, but being ensamples to the flock. And when the chief Shepherd shall appear, ye shall receive a crown of glory that fadeth not away" (1 Pet. 5:1-4)

"And when they had ordained them elders in every church, and had prayed with fasting, they commended them to the Lord, on whom they believed" (Acts 14:23).

"Is any sick among you? Let him call for the elders of the church; and let them pray over him, anointing him with oil in the name of the Lord: And the prayer of faith shall save the sick, and the Lord shall raise him up; and if he have committed sins, they shall be forgiven him" (Jas. 5:14-15).

There are twenty-four elders before the throne. In the Old Testament, there are twelve tribes of Israel and in the New Testament Jesus had twelve apostles. When Jesus arose from the dead, he transferred the Old Testament saints from paradise, a compartment of Sheol, into the presence of God.[2]

"Wherefore he saith, When he ascended up on high, he led captivity captive, and gave gifts unto men. (Now that he ascended, what is it but that he also descended first into the lower parts of the earth? He that descended is the same also that ascended up far above all heavens, that he might fill all things.)" (Eph. 4:8-10).

From that point on, when a New Testament saint dies, he or she immediately goes into the presence of the Lord in heaven.

"We are confident, I say, and willing rather to be absent from the body, and to be present with the Lord" (2 Cor. 5:8).

It is only the physical body that is buried. When Jesus appears, the dead in Christ from both Old and New Testament periods will be resurrected. We that are alive and remain will be caught up with them in the clouds to meet the Lord in the air.[3]

The twenty-four elders represent all the righteous in heaven. In chapter 4 verse 4 of the book of Revelation, John the revelator sees the crystal sea before the throne. This is not a body of water or large expanse of glass. In Scripture, a description of a mass of people accompanies the word "sea," whenever it is used without reference to the name or location of an existing body of water. The crystal sea is a great company of people standing before the throne of God. They are referred to as a sea because of their vast numbers and as crystal because of their right standing with God. Since the twenty-four elders are representatives, the Church whom they represent must also be in heaven. Thus, the crystal sea before the throne is the symbol of the entire Church company in heaven, and it is massive.[4]

There will definitely be a great end-time harvest of souls. Even though this harvest will be massive, many people will use their free will and choose to reject the Lord Jesus Christ.

"Say not ye, There are yet four months, and then cometh harvest? Behold, I say unto you, lift up your eyes, and look on the fields; for they are white already to harvest" (John 4:35).

To reach the vast sea of the masses of the unsaved throughout this planet, it is going to take a great deal of money. Not only will it take a great deal of money, but the wealth must be in the right hands.

"For whosoever shall call upon the name of the Lord shall be saved. How then shall they call on him in whom they have not believed? And how shall they believe in him of whom they have not heard? And how shall they hear without a preacher? And how shall they preach, except they be sent? As it is written, how beautiful are the feet of them that preach the gospel of peace, and bring glad tidings of good things!" (Rom. 10:13-15).

Let's continue with God's logic. Who will send a preacher other than God's people? I don't think that the devil's people will sponsor the preaching of the gospel. This requires action by God's people. How will God's people send the preacher unless they have wealth? The power to get wealth is to be used for God's glory.

CHAPTER TWO

END-TIME WEALTH TRANSFER

A great deal of financial wealth will be required to enable the Church to preach the gospel to all the nations so that billions of people can come into the kingdom of God. We will need to reach the unsaved through a variety of methods and media. We'll reach them through anointed preaching in traditional church services, through mission trips, conferences, seminars, books, e-books, downloads from websites, Internet radio, traditional radio, mailings, television, Internet videos, one-on-one witnessing, neighborhood outreaches, open-air meetings, tent meetings, tracks, CDs, DVDs and many other ways.

There is no doubt that it will take money placed in the right hands to reach those billions of lost people. The conversion of billions of souls will not take place if most of the wealth is in the hands of the lost or those unwilling to support the preaching of the gospel. Even if the wealth is primarily in the hands of the redeemed, this large influx into the kingdom of God will not be accomplished.

To accomplish such a task, the wealth will have to be in the hands of God's people who know what to do with it and who are not afraid to do what they know to do. Only those who live by kingdom principles will participate in God's end-time wealth transfer.

A transfer of wealth has always been available to God's people who could receive the revelation of this principle by faith. I believe this transfer will be accelerated in these last days.

"For God giveth to a man that is good in his sight wisdom, and knowledge, and joy: but to the sinner he giveth travail, to gather and to heap up, that he may give to him that is good before God" (Eccl. 2:26a).

"A good man leaveth an inheritance to his children's children: and the wealth of the sinner is laid up for the just" (Prov. 13:22).

"For thus saith the LORD of hosts; Yet once, it is a little while, and I will shake the heavens, and the earth, and the sea, and the dry land; And I will shake all nations, and the desire of all nations shall come: and I will fill this house with glory, saith the LORD of hosts. The silver is mine, and the gold is mine, saith the LORD of hosts. The glory of this latter house shall be greater than of the former, saith the LORD of hosts: and in this place will I give peace, saith the LORD of hosts" (Hag. 2:6-9).

Some people believe that the wealth transfer should come from those who have to those who have not. This is a counterfeit principle from Satan, and such a notion is contrary to the Word of God.

"And he said unto them that stood by, Take from him the pound, and give it to him that hath ten pounds. (And they said unto him, Lord, he hath ten pounds.) For I say unto you, That unto every one which hath shall be given; and from him that hath not, even that he hath shall be taken away from him" (Luke 19:24-26).

I believe that the accelerated end-time wealth transfer has, at the time of this writing, just entered its infant stage. For the full manifestation of this event, God's people must take dominion over time. (For further study on dominion over time, please see my book *Inhabiting Eternity on Earth*.) This transfer won't be from the rich to the poor; it won't even be from the lost to the saved. It will be from those who are afraid to work according to kingdom principles to those who are walking the narrow way, working according to kingdom principles, and thereby gaining by trading.

Let's study Luke 19:12-26 that reveals to us Jesus' parable of the ten pieces of money. The principles revealed in this parable have always existed and been vital for our prosperity in the Lord, but they are especially important in these last days. I will explain why later in this chapter.

"He said therefore, A certain nobleman went into a far country to receive for himself a kingdom, and to return. And he called his ten servants, and delivered them ten pounds, and said unto them, Occupy till I come. But his citizens hated him, and sent a message after him, saying, we will not have this man to reign over us" (Luke 19:12-14).

The certain nobleman is, of course, Jesus. He left this earth to receive his kingdom and he will someday return. His fellow earthly citizens indeed hated and rejected him.

"He came unto his own, and his own received him not" (John 1:11).

"He is despised and rejected of men; a man of sorrows, and acquainted with grief: and we hid as it were our faces from him; he was despised, and we esteemed him not" (Isa. 53:3).

Notice in the parable that the nobleman called his forth servants, not the ungodly. This parable is about God's people. Each servant got one pound, and each was to occupy or put the pounds to work until the nobleman's return.

"And it came to pass, that when he was returned, having received the kingdom, then he commanded these servants to be called unto him, to whom he had given the money, that he might know how much every man had gained by trading" (Luke 19:15).

Please notice that Jesus was talking about money. This parable is all about how we handle our money. One day, when Jesus returns, he is going to ask us about how we handled the money he gave us. Notice that he didn't ask how much money his servants had. He didn't asked how much they gained through the work of their hands. He wanted to know how much gain or increase they produced; and it wasn't just any increase, but how much they gained by trading. In other words, how much increase did they generate by investing the money that he had entrusted into their hands.

"Then came the first, saying, Lord, thy pound hath gained ten pounds. And he said unto him, Well, thou good servant: because thou hast been faithful in a very little, have thou authority over ten cities" (Luke 19:16-17).

Please notice the increase of ten pounds. When his master saw the increase, he was so pleased that he rewarded him directly proportional to his gain or increase.

"And the second came, saying, Lord, thy pound hath gained five pounds. And he said likewise to him, Be thou also over five cities" (Luke 19:18-19).

This servant was also rewarded according to the increase that he had developed through investing.

"And another came, saying, Lord, behold, here is thy pound, which I have kept laid up in a napkin: For I feared thee, because thou art an austere man: thou takest up that thou layedst not down, and reapest that thou didst not sow. And he saith unto him, Out of thine own mouth will I judge thee, thou wicked servant. Thou knewest that I was an austere man, taking up that I laid not down, and reaping that I did not sow" (Luke 19:20-22).

This servant did not invest because he was afraid. Fear is always the reason we don't invest. When we turn down an investment opportunity, it is because we are afraid that we will lose what we do have while we are trying to make a gain. Fear is the factor that stops investments. The servant feared out of a lack of knowledge and trust of the nobleman.

"Wherefore then gavest not thou my money into the bank, that at my coming I might have required mine own with usury?" (Luke 19:23).

Banks pay interest or "increase." Jesus is interested in increase, just as the nobleman was. He must be interested in us having an increase or he wouldn't have given his servants a city for every pound they gained.

"And he said unto them that stood by, Take from him the pound, and give it to him that hath ten pounds. (And they said unto him, Lord, he hath ten pounds)" (Luke 19:24-25).

Why didn't he give it to the one that gained five pounds? Here is the point that Jesus is making: The one that works his system the best is the one that receives what the man that walks in fear loses. The servants were shocked that the nobleman gave the non-invested pound to the one who had the most increase. The disciples needed their minds renewed in this area and so do many Christians. Remember, this parable was about God's servants spoken to God's servants. The disciples needed to understand the kingdom way of talking and doing things. Up to this time, the disciples had a "Robin Hood mentality," which they had to get rid of because it is a counterfeit way of thinking that originated from Satan. Jesus revealed his kingdom way of thinking to his servants.

"For I say unto you, That unto every one which hath shall be given; and from him that hath not, even that he hath shall be taken away from him" (Luke 19:26).

This is one of the God's kingdom principles that his people need to know and understand. It is a mystery to the ungodly.

"And the disciples came, and said unto him, Why speakest thou unto them in parables? He answered and said unto them, Because it is given unto you to know the mysteries of the kingdom of heaven, but to them it is not given. For whosoever hath, to him shall be given, and he shall have more abundance: but whosoever hath not, from him shall be taken away even that he hath. Therefore speak I to them in parables: because they seeing see not; and hearing they hear not, neither do they understand" (Matt. 13:10-13).

Don't think like the lost and miss out on the end-time wealth transfer. Jesus wants you to invest in the kingdom of God, and he guarantees you great increase and no chance of a loss, for the kingdom is good ground. No earthly endeavor can make such a promise.

"But other fell into good ground, and brought forth fruit, some an hundredfold, some sixtyfold, some thirtyfold. Who hath ears to hear, let him hear" (Matt. 13:8).

"But lay up for yourselves treasures in heaven, where neither moth nor rust doth corrupt, and where thieves do not break through nor steal" (Matt. 6:20).

Even servants of God who walk in fear are going to lose what Jesus is offering them, and it will go to the one who will walk in faith and believe for the increase. This is a principle that God has put into the earth. I'm not saying it's wrong to make an earthly investment. You will need those as you receive the supernatural increase or gain by trading from working this principle.

Let me explain it in detail. Let's read verse 26 again.

"For I say unto you, That unto every one which hath shall be given; and from him that hath not, even that he hath shall be taken away from him" (Luke 19:26).

How can someone who "hath not" have something taken away. What we have or have not is increase. That is what Jesus was talking about. What he wanted to know was this: how much every man gained by trading. In other words, Jesus will ask us how much increase we allowed him to give us by investing in the kingdom of God. In the way we talk today, the principle can be stated like this:

Everyone who has received increase through giving (investing) money into the kingdom of God will be given more money. This additional money will come from the ones who received no increase from God because they were afraid to put their money into the kingdom. The money they held back because of fear will go into the hands of those who know how to generate increase from God, so they can continue to support and advance God's kingdom.

In the lasts days, this "mystery" will be manifested through the acceleration of the production of the fruit of God's vineyards. That means that the time between sowing a seed and reaping a harvest will be shortened. As we obey God, we will be able to accomplish in a short time what used to take a much longer time. Partner with God, take dominion over time, and accomplish in one year what to the natural mind should take ten years. It's not too late for your dreams to come true.

"Behold, the days come, saith the LORD, that the plowman shall overtake the reaper, and the treader of grapes him that soweth seed; and the mountains shall drop sweet wine, and all the hills shall melt" (Amos 9:13).

I believe the days have come when the harvester comes right on the heels of the sower as we take dominion over time by faith. The plowman is making ready for new seeds on the heels of the reaper. Don't stop your faithfulness. Don't think you are too old for your dreams to come true. Realize that God has dominion over time and by faith so do you. Continue to dream big dreams. Now is not the time to quit; instead, go forward with renewed faith, for God has made a way for you to still fulfill your kingdom destiny.

The devil can't stop you. Your revelation of dominion over time beats his information about your age every time. Keep looking toward where you are going, continue to be faithful right where you are, sow more seeds than ever before. Don't quit, and the victory is automatically yours!

"And let us not be weary in well doing: for in due season we shall reap, if we faint not" (Gal. 6:9).

It is in the days described in Amos 9:13 that we find ourselves this very moment. God's end-time wealth transfer is in progress and accelerating. Notice that God's way of transfer is that money goes from the hands of the unproductive into the hands of the productive, just as it does in capitalism. It is not based on if you are in a special interest group. The basis for receiving is that you are a proven giver. God does not turn his back on the poor, for he has a special reward system for those who do good and give.

God's reward system is available to anyone who will work his system of sowing and reaping. No one is excluded. We are to give to get out the gospel to bring others into this marvelous kingdom of abundance. We are to give to those less fortunate than ourselves. God then rewards us for helping others.

"Give, and it shall be given unto you; good measure, pressed down, and shaken together, and running over, shall men give into your bosom. For with the same measure that ye mete withal it shall be measured to you again" (Luke 6:38).

The devil's counterfeit system helps one privileged group to the detriment of another group. God's wealth transfer helps those who receive and those who give. God's way is to bring everyone up to a high level of abundance. The problem is that not everyone will submit and think the way he thinks. There won't be equal outcomes, for he has given us free will, yet everyone has the opportunity to make it to the top. Satan's kingdom brings everyone down to the bottom together--the same principles you find in socialism.

"The thief cometh not, but for to steal, and to kill, and to destroy: I am come that they might have life, and that they might have it more abundantly. I am the good shepherd: the good shepherd giveth his life for the sheep" (John 10:10-11).

CHAPTER THREE

THE DEVIL'S COUNTERFEIT SYSTEM OF

WEALTH TRANSFER

Satan's counterfeit system for wealth transfer is nothing new. To find out what is happening today you can always look to history. Men who are truly wise find out what is happening today by studying what has already taken place in the Word of God.

"The thing that hath been, it is that which shall be; and that which is done is that which shall be done: and there is no new thing under the sun. Is there any thing whereof it may be said, See, this is new? it hath been already of old time, which was before us" (Eccl. 1:9-10).

"That which hath been is now; and that which is to be hath already been; and God requireth that which is past" (Eccl. 3:15).

The oldest recorded government-based wealth transfer is recorded in Genesis chapter 47. Everything valuable was moved from the hands of the people into the hands of the government. Godly wealth transfer always includes the kingdom of God's primary principle of sowing and reaping. Rather than trust God through sowing and reaping, the people of Egypt, through ignorance of

31

faith principles, chose to come to the Egyptian government for their needs to be met. After all, there was a global crisis, a food shortage. The supply of food kept going down yet the demand for food kept going up.

Eventually the people ran out of money. When supply is going down and demand is going up, or even remaining flat, there is inflation as prices "necessarily skyrocket." The people had to pay more money for the same amount of grain or get less grain for the same amount of money. Soon, their money ran out. Next, they gave up their livestock, and finally, they gave up 20 percent of their future production from the land.

They gave away part of their children's and grandchildren's futures in exchange for government protection in their present. Government seemed to have the answer to this global crisis and, as a result, gained control of all the people's possessions.

There were two groups, however, that did not suffer this indignity.

"And they said, Thou hast saved our lives: let us find grace in the sight of my lord, and we will be Pharaoh's servants. And Joseph made it a law over the land of Egypt unto this day, that Pharaoh should have the fifth part; except the land of the priests only, which became not Pharaoh's. And Israel dwelt in the land of Egypt, in the country of Goshen; and they had possessions therein, and grew, and multiplied exceedingly" (Gen. 47:25-27).

The priests were exempt from any payment to Pharaoh because they operated as willing partners. Please note that these priests were not priests associated with the God of Abraham, Isaac, and Jacob, but were men who proclaimed that Pharaoh was a god. They helped Pharaoh become the powerful man that he was and it was now time for their reward from Pharaoh. They agreed with the ideology of Pharaoh that government knows better what to do with your assets than you do. Pharaoh must take care of the priests to make sure they remain allies. This was necessary so the priests would continue to solidify Pharaoh's position of power for tomorrow just as they helped establish his position as a god already.

As king, Pharaoh used his authority over the people to take from one group and give it to the other group simply because they supported him and built him up as a god. The priests were given this reward even though they produced nothing. Pharaoh took from the producers and gave it to non-producers, because it was the non-producers who helped him gain his power.

Today, we have similar groups in the United States such as ACORN, government unions, SEIU, AFL-CIO, NPR, Planned Parenthood, New Black Panthers, and other like-minded groups. Not only do some of them get tax dollars, they also get preferential treatment. They receive such things as waivers from Obamacare. They receive exemption from prosecution by the Department of Justice, even when they commit crimes that the whole world can easily see and hear on video.

The other group that did not get in line for government assistance was God's people. Israel had the very best in all the land of Egypt. They had the best, but it was not because they worshipped Pharaoh. To the contrary, they had the best land all to themselves, with the ability to keep all they produced, and had great possessions, because they worshipped the God of Abraham.

They trusted in their God, the one true God. As a result, they had more than enough to freely help others. Helping others would be a decision that they could make of their own free will, not by edict of the government.

Pharaoh may have promoted the notion of how great government assistance can be. However, the people of Egypt did not survive the crisis because of Pharaoh or the government of Egypt. The people made it through the crisis because of Joseph. Egypt was not blessed because of its greatness. No, the people were rescued and had provision because of Joseph's relationship with God Almighty.

The people benefited from the faith, virtues, and principles that Joseph displayed. They received this benefit because it rains on the just and the unjust. Why was Joseph there? He was there so that in time of famine all Israel might be saved. The Egyptians just got the benefit of it.

"And Joseph said unto his brethren, I am Joseph; doth my father yet live? And his brethren could not answer him; for they were troubled at his presence. And Joseph said unto his brethren, Come near to me, I pray you. And they came near. And he said, I am Joseph your brother, whom ye sold into Egypt. Now therefore be not grieved, nor angry with yourselves, that ye sold me hither: for God did send me before you to preserve life. For these two years hath the famine been in the land: and yet there are five years, in the which there shall neither be earing nor harvest. And God sent me before you to preserve you a posterity in the earth, and to save your lives by a great deliverance" (Gen. 45:4-7).

Even with a decline in the acceptance of the greatness of the United States today, it is still, by far, the most blessed nation in the world. This nation is blessed, not because of atheists, socialists, communists, Marxists, Muslims and other folks who disrespect or hate the God of Abraham, Isaac, and Jacob. It is blessed because of God's people who desire to please him and operate according to

34

the principles of the kingdom of God. Because of God's people, we are the most giving, most generous nation in the history of the world. The people of our nation also have the highest standard of living in the world because it rains on the just and the unjust. The communists, socialists, and the rest of the folks outside of church of the Lord Jesus Christ get the benefit of great provision, opportunity, freedom, and liberty because of God's people.

"Now the Lord is that Spirit: and where the Spirit of the Lord is, there is liberty" (2 Cor. 3:17).

The Hebrews, God's people, were positioned in the land of Goshen, which was the best land in Egypt. They were not at all dependent on Pharaoh or the government. They had the best land and all of their possessions.

"And Joseph placed his father and his brethren, and gave them a possession in the land of Egypt, in the best of the land, in the land of Rameses, as Pharaoh had commanded. And Joseph nourished his father, and his brethren, and all his father's household, with bread, according to their families. And Israel dwelt in the land of Egypt, in the country of Goshen; and they had possessions therein, and grew, and multiplied exceedingly" (Gen. 47:11-12, 27).

The Hebrews had freedom and liberty to lead their lives as they saw fit. As they obeyed the laws of the one true God, they were a blessing to others. They were free to declare what the Spirit of the Lord was saying to them that they might fulfill their destiny to bless all the people of the earth because of the liberty they enjoyed. In such an environment of liberty, Jacob (Israel) spoke this blessing over his son Joseph.

"And Jacob said unto Joseph, God Almighty appeared unto me at Luz in the land of Canaan, and blessed me, and said unto me, Behold, I will make thee fruitful, and multiply thee, and I will make of thee a multitude of people; and will give this land to thy seed after thee for an everlasting possession (Gen. 48:4-5).

Jacob spoke the blessing of his grandfather Abraham over his son as it was an everlasting blessing. This blessing was not just for the people of Israel but for whosoever would receive it regardless of race, culture, gender, national origin or anything else. Everyone qualifies as a "whosoever."

"Now the LORD had said unto Abram, Get thee out of thy country, and from thy kindred, and from thy father's house, unto a land that I will shew thee: And I will make of thee a great nation, and I will bless thee, and make thy name great; and thou shalt be a blessing: And I will bless them that bless thee, and curse him that curseth thee: and in thee shall all families of the earth be blessed" (Gen.12:3).

"Therefore it is of faith, that it might be by grace; to the end the promise might be sure to all the seed; not to that only which is of the law, but to that also which is of the faith of Abraham; who is the father of us all, (As it is written, I have made thee a father of many nations,) before him whom he believed, even God, who quickeneth the dead, and calleth those things which be not as though they were. Who against hope believed in hope, that he might become the father of many nations; according to that which was spoken, So shall thy seed be. And being not weak in faith, he considered not his own body now dead, when he was about an hundred years old, neither yet the deadness of Sara's womb: He staggered not at the promise of God through unbelief; but was strong in faith, giving glory to God; And being fully persuaded that, what he had promised, he was able also to perform. And therefore it was imputed to him for righteousness. Now it was not written for his sake alone, that it was imputed to him; But for us also, to whom it shall be imputed, if we believe on him that raised up Jesus our Lord from the dead; Who was delivered for our offences, and was raised again for our justification" (Rom. 4:16-25).

"For ye are all the children of God by faith in Christ Jesus. For as many of you as have been baptized into Christ have put on Christ. There is neither Jew nor Greek, there is neither bond nor free, there is neither male nor female: for ye are all one in Christ Jesus. And if ye be Christ's, then are ye Abraham's seed, and heirs according to the promise" (Gal. 3:26-29).

Those who have entered into the family of God through faith in Christ Jesus have been grafted in to the good olive tree which is Israel.

"For if the firstfruit be holy, the lump is also holy: and if the root be holy, so are the branches. And if some of the branches be broken off, and thou, being a wild olive tree, wert graffed in among them, and with them partakest of the root and fatness of the olive tree" (Rom. 11:16-17).

"Wherefore remember, that ye being in time past Gentiles in the flesh, who are called Uncircumcision by that which is called the Circumcision in the flesh made by hands; That at that time ye were without Christ, being aliens from the commonwealth of Israel, and strangers from the covenants of promise, having no hope, and without God in the world: But now in Christ Jesus ye who sometimes were far off are made nigh by the blood of Christ. For he is our peace, who hath made both one, and hath broken down the middle wall of partition between us; Having abolished in his flesh the enmity, even the law of commandments contained in ordinances; for to make in himself of twain one new man, so making peace; And that he might reconcile both unto God in one body by the cross, having slain the enmity thereby: And came and preached peace to you which were afar off, and to them that were nigh. For through him we both have access by one Spirit unto the Father" (Eph. 2:11-18).

The Spirit of the Lord brings liberty. Liberty enables the people of God to walk in the blessings of Abraham to bless the whole world. Liberty brings blessings and a higher standard of living. Liberty is from God. Our founders knew this. God wants liberty for all people, but not all people will accept it. Because God gave us a free will, he cannot guarantee equal outcome for all people. God wants liberty, but people are free to reject the ways and thoughts of God. They think that they are smarter than God is; their foolishness is what brings people down to a lower level.

"I call heaven and earth to record this day against you, that I have set before you life and death, blessing and cursing: therefore choose life, that both thou and thy seed may live: That thou mayest love the LORD thy God, and that thou mayest obey his voice, and that thou mayest cleave unto him: for he is thy life, and the length of thy days: that thou mayest dwell in the land which the LORD sware unto thy fathers, to Abraham, to Isaac, and to Jacob, to give them" (Deut. 30:19-20).

Rebelling against God and thinking opposite from God not only brings you down but brings others down too as they are persuaded to think like a low-living, small-thinking, natural man. This will not bless others but rather brings failure, lack and even death.

"For my thoughts are not your thoughts, neither are your ways my ways, saith the LORD. For as the heavens are higher than the earth, so are my ways higher than your ways, and my thoughts than your thoughts" (Isa. 55:8-9).

"There is a way which seemeth right unto a man, but the end thereof are the ways of death" (Prov. 14:12 and 16:25).

All thinking contrary to the laws of God comes from our carnal nature or our flesh. There are those who proclaim they know better how to govern without regard to the laws of God. They think they should, for the most part, think for the people, without people having the liberty to think for themselves. These ruling elite believe they know what others should eat, what others should say, and even what kind of energy others should consume. They want their abundance to come from the backs of those who oppose them and from those who have been deceived into thinking they can't make it without government assistance. Those who believe they must have government assistance will continue to support the ones who promise greater assistance out of fear of losing their sustenance. Anything based on fear is not of God. God's kingdom is based on faith, not fear. This kind of fear does not come from God.

"For God hath not given us the spirit of fear; but of power, and of love, and of a sound mind" (2 Tim. 1:7).

Those who want to collapse the United States economy and its system of capitalism are carnally minded. They deceivingly state high moral intentions but really just want power. They don't care if the nation is destroyed and people suffer hardships, as long as they get power over people. They are deceived and mistakenly think that the wealth production will continue as before. They should

39

study history and find that every previous socialist nation has brought great poverty to its people and the government treasuries eventually end up empty.

All of that activity of planning the end of capitalism is demonic in its origin. We will discuss this at length later on. All of the socialistic forms of thinking and living that destroy liberty (communism, Marxism, liberation theology, Fabian Society, etc.) are contrary to the Word of God. They are from the flesh and they are carnal. To think in such a fashion is to be carnally minded.

"For they that are after the flesh do mind the things of the flesh; but they that are after the Spirit the things of the Spirit. For to be carnally minded is death; but to be spiritually minded is life and peace. Because the carnal mind is enmity against God: for it is not subject to the law of God, neither indeed can be. So then they that are in the flesh cannot please God" (Rom. 8:5-8).

Satan does not operate with original ideas and strategies. By the Spirit of God, we can discern his plan. At the time of this writing, Satan is implementing the beginning of his counterfeit wealth transfer system.

"Lest Satan should get an advantage of us: for we are not ignorant of his devices" (2 Cor. 2:11).

If Satan's is accelerating his counterfeit wealth transfer, then that means that God has begun his accelerated end-time wealth transfer system to finance his end-time transfer of souls from the kingdom of darkness into the Kingdom of Light. Nobody ever counterfeits anything unless it is real and it has great value. You won't ever see a counterfeit $400 bill or a counterfeit $1 bill. Why? There is no real $400 bill and the $1 bill has little value.

Satan's wealth transfer plan is solely based on fear and has nothing to do with faith. It is strictly for the benefit of a few and not designed to bless everyone. God's wealth transfer as explained in Chapter 2 is based on faith and is designed to bless whosoever will. The benefits are not exclusionary and the blessings are not designed for just certain groups in power.

Our heavenly Father does not want his children to look to the government to take care of them. We are his people and he is our sole source of supply.

"But my God shall supply all your need according to his riches in glory by Christ Jesus" (Phil. 4:19).

"Therefore take no thought, saying, What shall we eat? or, What shall we drink? or, Wherewithal shall we be clothed? (For after all these things do the Gentiles seek :) for your heavenly Father knoweth that ye have need of all these things. But seek ye first the kingdom of God, and his righteousness; and all these things shall be added unto you" (Matt. 6:31-33).

One last thought on Pharaoh's government-based wealth-transfer system. Have you ever thought of what would happen if the people of Egypt had refused to give Pharaoh the 20 percent? They would be in default and could be evicted from their land. Don't be surprised if you hear discussions from the progressive moment to solve our deficit through a federal wealth tax on people's property to effect an ungodly, evil redistribution of wealth.

CHAPTER FOUR

WEALTH TRANSFERS IN SCRIPTURE

Remember, there is nothing new under the sun. Godly wealth transfer and ungodly counterfeit wealth transfer have been in play since the beginning. God blessed Adam and Eve and put them in the Garden of Eden, a wealthy place. But Satan robbed Adam and Eve of that wealth with his lies and temptations. Satan is likewise trying to rob us of the blessings and the abundance from God.

If we want to know what God's desire is for us today, we can see what it was from the very beginning, because he never changes. Let's examine God's plan vs. the devil's tactics beginning at Creation.

Imagine how God felt when man, immediately after receiving life, looked back into the face of God. I imagine that it would be very similar to the way a mother feels when she first holds her newborn and that baby looks back into his or her mother's eyes. Out of the depth of their mutual being comes a tremendous love and intimacy. God's love and desire for intimacy with us is even greater than a mother's with her child.

"Can a woman forget her suckling child, that she should not have compassion on the son of her womb? Yea, they may forget, yet will I not forget thee" (Isa. 49:15).

The first thing God did after creating man was to place him in a beautiful garden, in paradise. It was paradise because there were no worries, just like in heaven. God still wants it today on earth as it is in heaven, so he invites us to cast all of our cares on him.

"And the LORD God formed man out of the dust of the ground, and breathed into his nostrils the breath of life; and man became a living soul. And the LORD God planted a garden eastward in Eden; and there he put the man whom he had formed" (Gen. 2:7-8).

So immediately after giving life to man, God placed man in a beautiful garden where there was the same love and harmony out of which God had formed and created man. In the Garden of Eden, there was no discord, no sin, no sickness—nothing that would bring unrest. There was only peace, joy, communication, and fellowship between God and man. From the start, God extended his goodness toward man on earth. God showed his love and trust by placing Adam in the garden and giving him dominion over everything in the garden, even the fruit of the trees. Except one. In order for man to be man, he had to be able to say yes or no. Man had to be able to respond to and react to God by his own choices.

God doesn't want robots. Neither do we want robots for children. I remember when my two children were young. When I came home from work, no matter what they were doing, they would run to greet me, throw their arms around my neck, and tell me that they love me. That brought great joy to me. It was and still is more precious than anything that money can buy.

What if instead of running to greet me, my children just sat in place watching television. If I would have to threaten them to get them to say they love me, to honor me, and to obey my words, it just wouldn't be the same. I want a real love that comes from their choice to love me. God wants the same thing from us, his children.

The devil, in the form of a serpent, knew that man had to make a choice to follow God or to be a god unto himself. Satan then planted the seed of doubt in man's mind—to doubt the goodness of God.

"Now the serpent was more subtil than any beast of the field which the LORD God had made. And he said unto the woman, Yea, hath God said, ye shall not eat of every tree of the garden? And the woman said unto the serpent, We may eat of the fruit of the trees of the garden: But of the fruit of the tree which is in the midst of the garden, God hath said, Ye shall not eat of it, neither shall ye touch it, lest ye die. And the serpent said unto the woman, Ye shall not surely die: For God doth know that in the day ye eat thereof, then your eyes shall be opened, and ye shall be as gods, knowing good and evil. And when the woman saw that the tree was good for food, and that it was pleasant to the eyes, and a tree to be desired to make one wise, she took of the fruit thereof, and did eat, and gave also unto her husband with her; and he did it. And the eyes of them both were opened, and they knew that they were naked; and they sewed fig leaves together, and made themselves aprons" (Gen. 3:1-7).

God has a good plan for your life and the devil has an evil plan for your life. It is up to you to choose. Jesus shed his blood and died for whosoever will enter in to a blood covenant with him and become a joint heir with him as a child of the king. Each one of us must accept or reject the blood covenant.

When God's people trusted Satan's lies more than the promises of God, the world system began. When Adam sinned, he lost his connection to God just as if an electric cord was unplugged from the wall socket. He was driven out of the garden and he lost his assignment, his authority, and his provision. His provision was now cursed. He couldn't operate in the Kingdom of God. He had to operate in a cursed world system for his provision.

"And unto Adam he said, Because thou hast hearkened unto the voice of thy wife, and hast eaten of the tree, of which I commanded thee, saying, Thou shalt not eat of it: cursed is the ground for thy sake; in sorrow shalt thou eat of it all the days of thy life; Thorns also and thistles shall it bring forth to thee; and thou shalt eat the herb of the field; in the sweat of thy face shalt thou eat bread, till thou return unto the ground; for out of it wast thou taken: for dust thou art, and unto dust shalt thou return" (Gen. 3:17-19).

Man became a survivor with the mentality that he must do whatever it takes to survive and to provide for his family. That "whatever" usually means by the sweat of his brow or by stepping on someone else to get to the top. Man entered the devil's world system—a system based on fear. Satan uses that fear to manipulate people to do his will and perform evil acts without regard for others.

Jesus of Nazareth, "the last Adam" (1 Cor. 15:45), came to earth, redeemed mankind, and restored lost humanity to our rightful place. He came to take the toil out of life, replacing it with a life of abundance though an assignment from God and the authority to complete it. Jesus lived a life without sin, was crucified on the cross for our sins, was buried, and rose again from the dead. He took on the devil, and as we say here in Texas, he put a "whuppin" on him. It was a complete and total defeat.

Jesus took back everything, wealth included, that Satan had stolen. He took everything including the spoil and made a way for us, in his name, to take the spoil from the devil when he steals from us.

"Blotting out the handwriting of ordinances that was against us, which was contrary to us, and took it out of the way, nailing it to his cross; And having spoiled principalities and powers, he made a shew of them openly, triumphing over them in it" (Col. 2:14-15).

Taking spoil from the enemies of God is normal for God's victorious people throughout Scripture. Through faith in God, we activate God's wealth transfer system. The more Satan oppresses God's people, the bigger the "whuppin" he is going to have to take and the more spoil he will have to lose to those who trust God.

Godly wealth transfer takes place when people activate the giving principle as demonstrated in Luke chapter 19. We are free to do this anytime we want. I'm talking about sowing in good soil for the sake of the gospel, not giving to an organization like Planned Parenthood and calling it a "charitable" contribution.

In addition, godly wealth transfer takes place when God's people believe God to take back what the devil has stolen. When it is not only believed for, but also acted on, God gives his people complete victory over the enemy and generous spoil on top of the recovery.

Let's consider the children of Israel in Egypt. They were prospering in the land of Goshen as they lived the way God told them to live (not as the world lived). Many times in Scripture, we see a common cycle for God's people. They obey God and prosper greatly. Then they turn their eyes more on the blessing than on the One who blesses. They end up merging and mixing with the ways of the world. They introduce the world's "gods" into their homes, and it becomes hard to tell God's people from the rest. Eventually, they fall into bondage to the world. In despair, they turn to God, prosper, and the cycle begins again.

Such was the case of God's people in Egypt. Rather than continuing to influence the Egyptians, they were being influenced by the Egyptians. Not only had they been living in Egypt all those years, but, for a long time, Egypt had been living in them. They found themselves in bondage to the taskmasters of Pharaoh and had lost their liberty. They had been on the wrong end of another government-based, ungodly wealth transfer. This time, the Israelites conformed to the world and were subject to government oppression. It was much worse than before because this Pharaoh didn't know Joseph.

"Now there arose up a new king over Egypt, which knew not Joseph" (Exod. 1:8).

There is no way that Pharaoh didn't know who Joseph was. Everybody in Egypt knew about Joseph and how he saved the people. This Pharaoh had no regard for Joseph's God, Joseph's culture, Joseph's people, or Joseph's principles. It was Joseph's eighty-year use of the principles from the God of Abraham, Isaac, and Jacob that built Egypt into the most powerful nation on the earth. Subsequently, Pharaoh became the most powerful man on the earth.

Pharaoh was changing Egypt, but not for the better. Pharaoh was bringing about "change" and "fundamentally transforming" the most powerful nation in the world. It had become the most powerful nation in the world because of God's principles, modeled by his people. Pharaoh changed Egypt into a nation that oppressed the people of the God of Abraham, and that surely brought destruction to the nation.

The same thing will happen to the United States of America if the church of Jesus Christ doesn't stand up and declare that this nation should submit to the God of Abraham and refuse to bow and cater to the culture of Allah. We need the truth, not political correctness. Hidden and diluted truth takes away people's liberty; the elevating and promotion of truth brings liberty. It's only the truth you know that makes you free.

"And ye shall know the truth, and the truth shall make you free" (John 8:32).

The more Pharaoh oppressed the Hebrews, the bigger fall he was headed for when God's people finally turned to God. After Pharaoh's Egypt was riddled by plagues, Pharaoh lost his first born son and finally said to Moses that the Hebrews could leave.

God not only set his people free to live in the land of promise, but he caused his people to leave Egypt with spoil. They stripped the Egyptians of their wealth. Anytime we leave Egypt (come out of the world system) we receive a total victory. It might look shaky for a while, but if we stand on God's Word, we will rout the enemy and collect the spoil.

The following verses show how the children of Israel obeyed God and took spoil right from the hands of the Egyptians. The wealth moved from the hands of those in the world system into the hands of God's obedient servants. Note that the Hebrew word *shaal* is incorrectly translated as "borrow" in the King James Version in the verses below. *Shaal* means to ask, request, demand or require. The Israelites asked or demanded the spoil and the Egyptians complied as they thought of the miracles performed on the behalf of God's people.

"And I will give this people favour in the sight of the Egyptians: and it shall come to pass, that, when ye go, ye shall not go empty: But every woman shall borrow of her neighbour, and of her that sojourneth in her house, jewels of silver, and jewels of gold, and raiment: and ye shall put them upon your sons, and upon your daughters; and ye shall spoil the Egyptians" (Exod. 3:21-22).

"And the LORD said unto Moses, Yet will I bring one plague more upon Pharaoh, and upon Egypt; afterwards he will let you go hence: when he shall let you go, he shall surely thrust you out hence altogether. Speak now in the ears of the people, and let every man borrow of his neighbour, and every woman of her neighbour, jewels of silver, and jewels of gold. And there shall be a great cry throughout all the land of Egypt, such as there was none like it, nor shall be like it any more. But against any of the children of Israel shall not a dog move his tongue, against man or beast: that ye may know how that the LORD doth put a difference between the Egyptians and Israel" (Exod. 11:1-2, 6-7).

Whenever we decide to come out of the world system and think and live according to God's principles, our enemy will try to instill fear in us, hoping we will want to turn around and go back. The world system is based on controlling people through fear. If we stand strong and call on the name of the Lord, we shall experience utter and complete victory along with our spoil.

"And when Pharaoh drew nigh, the children of Israel lifted up their eyes, and, behold, the Egyptians marched after them; and they were sore afraid: and the children of Israel cried out unto the LORD. And they said unto Moses, because there were no graves in

Egypt, hast thou taken us away to die in the wilderness? Wherefore hast thou dealt thus with us, to carry us forth out of Egypt? Is not this the word that we did tell thee in Egypt, saying, Let us alone, that we may serve the Egyptians? For it had been better for us to serve the Egyptians, than that we should die in the wilderness. And Moses said unto the people, Fear ye not, stand still, and see the salvation of the LORD, which he will shew to you to day: for the Egyptians whom ye have seen to day, ye shall see them again no more for ever. The LORD shall fight for you, and ye shall hold your peace" (Exod. 14:10-14).

Iran and other nations that want to destroy Israel should think twice about attacking Israel. They should remember the Six Day War. They have been so deceived by the devil that they are blinded by hate and foolishness. My advice to them is this: Don't mess with Israel.

"And Moses stretched forth his hand over the sea, and the sea returned to his strength when the morning appeared; and the Egyptians fled against it; and the LORD overthrew the Egyptians in the midst of the sea. And the waters returned, and covered the chariots, and the horsemen, and all the host of Pharaoh that came into the sea after them; there remained not so much as one of them. But the children of Israel walked upon dry land in the midst of the sea; and the waters were a wall unto them on their right hand, and on their left. Thus the LORD saved Israel that day out of the hand of the Egyptians; and Israel saw the Egyptians dead upon the sea shore. And Israel saw that great work which the LORD did upon the Egyptians: and the people feared the LORD, and believed the LORD, and his servant Moses" (Exod. 14:27-31).

Another example of godly wealth transfer from the wicked to those who please God is found in the book of Second Chronicles. It is interesting to note that the wealth always leaves those who come against Israel. Remember that those of us that are in Christ have been grafted into the nation of Israel, and the blessing of Abraham is upon us.

"Then there came some that told Jehoshaphat, saying, There cometh a great multitude against thee from beyond the sea on this side Syria; and, behold, they be Hazazon-tamar, which is En-gedi. And Jehoshaphat feared, and set himself to seek the LORD, and proclaimed a fast throughout all Judah" (2 Chron. 20:2-3).

Currently, Israel is surrounded by enemies. They are surrounded by enemies of God who want the destruction of Israel, the United States, all Christians, and freedom. They want to eliminate freedom because in an environment of liberty, people are free to pursue their God-given vision and their kingdom destiny. Freedom enables us to grow strong in the power of his might. Our founders called this the "pursuit of happiness." Israel's current situation is not as bad (yet) as it was in Second Chronicles chapter 20. Let's see what happened.

"And now, behold, the children of Ammon and Moab and mount Seir, whom thou wouldest not let Israel invade, when they came out of the land of Egypt, but they turned from them, and destroyed them not; Behold, I say, how they reward us, to come to cast us out of thy possession, which thou hast given us to inherit. O our God, wilt thou not judge them? For we have no might against this great company that cometh against us; neither know we what to do: but our eyes are upon thee. And all Judah stood before the LORD, with their little ones, their wives, and their children. Then upon Jahaziel the son of Zechariah, the son of Benaiah, the son of Jeiel, the son of Mattaniah, a Levite of the sons of Asaph, came the Spirit of the LORD in the midst of the congregation; And he said, Hearken ye, all Judah, and ye inhabitants of Jerusalem, and thou king Jehoshaphat, Thus saith the LORD unto you, Be not afraid nor dismayed by reason of this great multitude; for the battle is not yours, but God's. To morrow go ye down against them: behold, they come up by the cliff of Ziz; and ye shall find them at the end of the brook, before the wilderness of Jeruel. Ye shall not need to fight in this battle: set yourselves, stand ye still, and see the salvation of the LORD with you, O Judah and Jerusalem: fear not, nor be dismayed; to morrow go out against them: for the LORD will be with you" (2 Chron. 2:10-17).

Israel today is much better equipped with a modern weaponry advantage. In addition, with God on their side, it doesn't matter what the odds appear to be in the natural. Again, my advice to Iran and others: Don't mess with Israel.

"And they rose early in the morning, and went forth into the wilderness of Tekoa: and as they went forth, Jehoshaphat stood and said, Hear me, O Judah, and ye inhabitants of Jerusalem; Believe in the LORD your God, so shall ye be established; believe his prophets, so shall ye prosper. And when he had consulted with the people, he appointed singers unto the LORD, and that should praise the beauty of holiness, as they went out before the army, and to say, Praise the LORD; for his mercy endureth for ever. And when they began to sing and to praise, the LORD set ambushments against the children of Ammon, Moab, and mount Seir, which were come against Judah; and they were smitten. For the children of Ammon and Moab stood up against the inhabitants of mount Seir, utterly to slay and destroy them: and when they had made an end of the inhabitants of Seir, every one helped to destroy another. And when Judah came toward the watch tower in the wilderness, they looked unto the multitude, and, behold, they were dead bodies fallen to the earth, and none escaped. And when Jehoshaphat and his people came to take away the spoil of them, they found among them in abundance both riches with the dead bodies, and precious jewels, which they stripped off for themselves, more than they could carry away: and they were three days in gathering of the spoil, it was so much." (2 Chron. 20:20-24).

It took *three days* to carry off the spoil because it was so much. I love God's wealth distribution plan. I hate the devil's government-based, global wealth redistribution. The more global the plan is in nature, the more evil it is. We will examine this in depth in chapter 5.

Let's look at one more example of God's wealth redistribution plan due to God's people being ripped off by the world system.

"And it came to pass, when David and his men were come to Ziklag on the third day, that the Amalekites had invaded the south, and Ziklag, and smitten Ziklag, and burned it with fire; and had taken the women captives, that were therein: they slew not any, either great or small, but carried them away, and went on their way. So David and his men came to the city, and, behold, it was burned with fire; and their wives, and their sons, and their daughters, were taken captives. Then David and the people that were with him lifted up their voice and wept, until they had no more power to weep. And David said to Abiathar the priest, Ahimelech's son, I pray thee, bring me hither the ephod. And Abiathar brought thither the ephod to David. And David inquired at the LORD, saying, Shall I pursue after this troop? Shall I overtake them? And he answered him, Pursue: for thou shalt surely overtake them, and without fail recover all" (1 Sam. 30:1-4, 7-8).

David and his men pursued and found an Egyptian, a servant to an Amalekite, who was left behind because he was sick. This man told David that it was the Amelekites that had burned and plundered Ziglag. He also told David that he could bring David and his men down to the Amalekites' camp. In Scripture, the Amalekites always represent the enemies of God. Let's see what happened next.

"And when he had brought him down, behold, they were spread abroad upon all the earth, eating and drinking, and dancing, because of all the great spoil that they had taken out of the land of the Philistines, and out of the land of Judah. And David smote them from the twilight even unto the evening of the next day: and there escaped not a man of them, save four hundred young men, which rode upon camels, and fled. And David recovered all that the Amalekites had carried away: and David rescued his two wives. And there was nothing lacking to them, neither small nor great, neither sons nor daughters, neither spoil, nor any thing that they had taken to them: David recovered all. And David took all the flocks and the herds, which they drave before those other cattle, and said, This is David's spoil" (1 Sam. 30:16-20).

David identified his enemy. If you fail to identify your enemy, things will get worse instead of better. People are not our enemy. If we come against people, the devil will have more opportunities to steal from us. David identified his enemy in verses 13-14. He found out that the Amalekites had burned Ziklag with fire and stolen his family and belongings. We can only recover what was stolen from the person who has stolen from us. The devil is our enemy, and he is the one who steals from us.

"The thief cometh not, but for to steal, and to kill, and to destroy" (John 10: 10a).

Command the enemy to give back what he has stolen. We need to know that he is afraid of the Jesus in us. We should use the name of Jesus and let God's power do the work.

"Recompense to no man evil for evil. Provide things honest in the sight of all men. If it be possible, as much as lieth in you, live peaceably with all men. Dearly beloved, avenge not yourselves, but rather give place unto wrath: for it is written, Vengeance is mine; I will repay, saith the Lord. Therefore if thine enemy hunger, feed him; if he thirst, give him drink: for in so doing thou shalt heap coals of fire on his head. Be not overcome of evil, but overcome evil with good" (Rom. 12: 17–21).

God's Word instructs us not to come against people. People are not our enemy. We should love people, even those who harm us, but we should show no mercy to the devil and his forces. When the enemy steals from us, we should make him pay and take spoil.

"For we wrestle not against flesh and blood, but against principalities, against powers, against the rulers of the darkness of this world, against spiritual wickedness in high places" (Eph. 6: 12).

You don't want to miss out on being included on the receiving end of our victories. Sow generously into the kingdom of God; make God the source of your provision. Believe his prophets, put your eyes on God, expect the increase, and be looking for the spoil.

CHAPTER FIVE

GETTING OUT OF THE WORLD SYSTEM

"This know also, that in the last days perilous times shall come. For men shall be lovers of their own selves, covetous, boasters, proud, blasphemers, disobedient to parents, unthankful, unholy, without natural affection, trucebreakers, false accusers, incontinent, fierce, despisers of those that are good, traitors, heady, highminded, lovers of pleasures more than lovers of God; having a form of godliness, but denying the power thereof: from such turn away" (2 Tim. 3:1-5).

The above Scriptures describe the world in which we live today—a place full of things that can bring fear into our lives. That's just what the devil wants. It seems that the world has been turned upside down and people in positions of authority are calling evil good and good evil. Some seem to advocate violence. I'm talking about the heads of unions and presidential appointees as "czars." Some of these people with official positions in the United States government openly praise violence and socialism and routinely bash capitalism. This would have been deemed impossible just a few short years ago.

Things seem to be getting worse. We can be sure we are in "the last days" by looking at other Scriptures as well as the one above. Many people disregard the ways of God and bring down our society, but they are without excuse.

"For I am not ashamed of the gospel of Christ: for it is the power of God unto salvation to every one that believeth; to the Jew first, and also to the Greek. For therein is the righteousness of God revealed from faith to faith: as it is written, the just shall live by faith. For the wrath of God is revealed from heaven against all ungodliness and unrighteousness of men, who hold the truth in unrighteousness; because that which may be known of God is manifest in them; for God hath shewed it unto them. For the invisible things of him from the creation of the world are clearly seen, being understood by the things that are made, even his eternal power and Godhead; so that they are without excuse: Because that, when they knew God, they glorified him not as God, neither were thankful; but became vain in their imaginations, and their foolish heart was darkened. Professing themselves to be wise, they became fools, And changed the glory of the uncorruptible God into an image made like to corruptible man, and to birds, and fourfooted beasts, and creeping things. Wherefore God also gave them up to uncleanness through the lusts of their own hearts, to dishonour their own bodies between themselves: Who changed the truth of God into a lie, and worshipped and served the creature more than the Creator, who is blessed for ever. Amen. For this cause God gave them up unto vile affections: for even their women did change the natural use into that which is against nature: And likewise also the men, leaving the natural use of the woman, burned in their lust one toward another; men with men working that which is unseemly, and receiving in themselves that recompence of their error which was meet. And even as they did not like to retain God in their knowledge, God gave them over to a reprobate mind, to do those things which are not convenient; being filled with all unrighteousness, fornication, wickedness, covetousness, maliciousness; full of envy, murder, debate, deceit, malignity; whisperers, backbiters, haters of God, despiteful, proud, boasters, inventors of evil things, disobedient to parents, Without understanding, covenant breakers, without natural affection, implacable, unmerciful: Who knowing the judgment of God, that they which commit such things are worthy of death, not only do the same, but have pleasure in them that do them" (Rom. 1:16-32).

Those Scriptures make me think of many people in politics today, especially the phrase "professing themselves to be wise, they became fools." It's almost unbelievable to hear a so-called "expert" in legislation say that we have to pass the bill to see what's in the bill. This is not what our founders, who were, for the most part, spirit-led men of God, had in mind when they fashioned the Bill of Rights and our wonderful U.S. Constitution.

There will not be a good outcome for those who think their ways are smarter and better than the God of Israel's. It is wise to yield to God, receive his son Jesus, become born again, and be grafted in to the spiritual nation of Israel. All the hate that has been increasingly manifested in the nations of the world is based on hating the people and nation of Israel. I will continue to show you, through godly principles, that Jesus is a capitalist. However, the greatest evidence is this. Every nation that hates Israel also hates capitalism. Virtually every person that hates Israel also hates capitalism. Virtually every person that hates capitalism also hates the United States. Virtually every person that teaches people to hate Israel also teaches people to hate capitalism and the United States. For example, Muslim militants call the United States the great Satan and call Israel little Satan.

As children of God, we don't have to depend on the government to survive. Jacob (whose name was changed to Israel) and his family prospered. "They had possessions therein, and grew, and multiplied exceedingly" (Gen. 47:27). This is a picture of how the people of God should live today, even while living in the middle of an evil, satanic, wealth redistribution plan.

Even though Jacob and his family were in Egypt, they did not think and live like the people of Egypt (the world). They were in the world but not of the world. They had separated themselves from the Egyptians and did not embrace the culture and the gods of Egypt.

"And what agreement hath the temple of God with idols? For ye are the temple of the living God; as God hath said, I will dwell in them, and walk in them; and I will be their God, and they shall be my people. Wherefore come out from among them, and be ye separate, saith the Lord, and touch not the unclean thing; and I will receive you, And will be a Father unto you, and ye shall be my sons and daughters, saith the Lord Almighty" (2 Cor. 6:17-18).

As we no longer conform to the world, no longer think, talk and act like the rest of the world but instead think, talk, and act like God, we too will prosper, even in the worst economy that there is.

"And be not conformed to this world: but be ye transformed by the renewing of your mind, that ye may prove what is that good, and acceptable, and perfect, will of God" (Rom. 12:2).

Our minds have to be renewed. We are first of this world, and then we are born again into the kingdom of God. But we still try to operate with the thinking of this world, and we fail. Jesus is first of the kingdom of God, was born into this world, and operated with the thinking and knowledge of the kingdom of God. Therefore, he was perfect in every way.

"Let this mind be in you, which was also in Christ Jesus" (Phil. 2: 5).

The apostle Paul instructs us to put on the mind of Christ. If our thinking starts to change, we will change.

"For as he thinketh in his heart, so is he" (Prov. 23: 7a).

They way we think and the knowledge of the goodness of God is the key to the way we live, because we are what we think. We can either think like man and fail or think like God and have success. When we think differently, we will talk differently.

"For out of the abundance of the heart the mouth speaketh" (Matt. 12: 34b).

What we think in our heart will come out of our mouth. It's just like a tube of toothpaste. When pressure is applied, the contents come out. Sometimes God will allow a little pressure to test us, so we can see what is in our heart by what comes out of our mouth. We must be careful what we speak, because what we speak sets our life, and we speak what we think.

"A man shall be satisfied with good by the fruit of his mouth" (Prov. 12:14a).

"A man's belly shall be satisfied with the fruit of his mouth; and with the increase of his lips shall he be filled. Death and life are in the power of the tongue: and they that love it shall eat the fruit thereof" (Prov. 18: 20–21).

If you start to think like God, you will begin to talk like God. God talks differently than man. God uses the creative power of the spoken word to manifest in the natural what he has believed in his heart. As children of God who are made in the image of God, we too have creative power with our words. We should operate as our heavenly Father to speak with our mouths what we believe in our hearts, so that what we believe might be manifest in the natural for the glory of God.

"(As it is written, I have made thee a father of many nations,) before him whom he believed, even God, who quickeneth the dead, and calleth those things which be not as though they were" (Rom. 4:17).

God created the world with his words, and we create our world with our words. That's why we should think in our hearts like God thinks, because what is in our hearts will come out of our mouths, and what comes out of our mouths will create our world.

Right thinking produces right living. Transformed thinking produces transformed living.
If we are transformed to live like God on the earth because we renew our minds, then we will have the same motives as Jesus to go about doing good, healing all who are oppressed of the devil, and seeking to save those who are lost. Without the knowledge of the goodness of God, we can be tormented and even destroyed. But the knowledge of the goodness of God can give us everything good, including the life of God.

"According as his divine power hath given unto us all things that pertain unto life and godliness, through the knowledge of him that hath called us to glory and virtue" (2 Pet. 1: 3).

God wants us to think on good things, which eventually bless people. The devil wants you to think on evil things, which eventually harm people.

"Finally, brethren, whatsoever things are true, whatsoever things are honest, whatsoever things are just, whatsoever things are pure, whatsoever things are lovely, whatsoever things are of good report; if there be any virtue, and if there be any praise, think on these things" (Phil. 4:8).

All throughout history, people have rebelled against God and thought that their way of thinking was better than God's way of thinking. Wrong thinking produces wrong decisions that produce wrong consequences. They blame God, and then they decide to reach their goals without God and in opposition to God. Again, there is nothing new under the sun. We find people who think they don't need God in Genesis chapter 11.

"And the whole earth was of one language, and of one speech. And it came to pass, as they journeyed from the east, that they found a plain in the land of Shinar; and they dwelt there. And they said one to another, Go to, let us make brick, and burn them throughly. And they had brick for stone, and slime had they for morter. And they said, Go to, let us build us a city and a tower, whose top may reach unto heaven; and let us make us a name, lest we be scattered abroad upon the face of the whole earth. And the LORD came down to see the city and the tower, which the children of men builded. And the LORD said, Behold, the people is one, and they have all one language; and this they begin to do: and now nothing will be restrained from them, which they have imagined to do. Go to, let us go down, and there confound their language, that they may not understand one another's speech. So the LORD scattered them abroad from thence upon the face of all the earth: and they left off to build the city. Therefore is the name of it called Babel; because the LORD did there confound the language of all the earth: and from thence did the LORD scatter them abroad upon the face of all the earth" (Gen. 11:1-9).

Ever since the fall of Adam and Eve, man has wanted to unite and strive against God. All throughout history, evil men have desired to create a new world order or an open society without borders and without individual nations. God has continually resisted this because he has his own plan. Many men in their own pride want to have all men alike without recognizing man's diversity and the uniqueness of each individual. God resisted man's pride in his own achievements, which was represented by the Tower of Babel.

"But he giveth more grace. Wherefore he saith, God resisteth the proud, but giveth grace unto the humble" (Jas. 4:6).

After the flood, God gave the same instructions to Noah that he gave to Adam. God wanted his people to spread out over the earth to subdue it and take dominion over it for his glory.

"And God blessed Noah and his sons, and said unto them, Be fruitful, and multiply, and replenish the earth. And the fear of you and the dread of you shall be upon every beast of the earth, and upon every fowl of the air, upon all that moveth upon the earth, and upon all the fishes of the sea; into your hand are they delivered. Every moving thing that liveth shall be meat for you; even as the green herb have I given you all things" (Gen. 9:1-3).

By the eleventh chapter of the book of Genesis, we see that man has not obeyed God by setting out to replenish the earth but has, instead, migrated to gather together in one place. They were all together and had one language. God confused their language and forced them to scatter across the face of the earth as he had originally intended.

If God had not dispersed them through the confusion of their language, most of the entire population would have ended up working for the Babylonian government, building the devil's system, and working for slave-like wages to fulfill the vision of a few ruling elite.

What did the Babylonian system want to do? Verse 4 of chapter 11 tells that they wanted to build a city, build a tower in that city that reached to heaven, make a name for themselves, and not to be scattered across the earth. Building a city was just a way not to be dispersed. Building a tower to reach heaven is just a way to make a name for themselves. Both of these goals were totally opposite of the will of God then and are still in rebellion against God today.

Making a name is all about regarding the approval of men more than the approval of God. If they valued the approval of God, they would have dispersed to replenish the earth. They built a city so that they wouldn't have to disperse. They needed the security of man rather than trust the goodness and faithfulness of God. Dispersing meant leaving the security of man and trusting in God for their security. They would have to leave the common provision and seek their own kingdom destiny. Little did they know that the common provision is the lowest level of provision that there is. For after the ruling elite get their share, there is very little left to share in common. They didn't realize that God had a unique, wonderful plan to profit each one of them.

"For I know the thoughts that I think toward you, saith the LORD, thoughts of peace, and not of evil, to give you an expected end" (Jer. 29:11).

The devil never wants man to realize the plan of God that stems from the uniqueness of each person. Any natural father can tell you that each of his children is different, yet he loves each one. The Tower of Babel symbolized the devil's desire to recognize no difference between individuals. This is similar to the way most unions operate. The union eliminates risk for the workers as everyone gets the same deal. Those with unique abilities to excel are encouraged to slack off, because everyone is expected to work with the same abilities and at the same pace.

The tower was to be built with bricks. Each brick looked exactly like the other bricks. There was no uniqueness in the materials. The devil, through Pharaoh, had God's people make bricks in Egypt. He didn't want them to recognize their uniqueness and how special they were to God.

"And the Egyptians made the children of Israel to serve with rigour: And they made their lives bitter with hard bondage, in morter, and in brick, and in all manner of service in the field: all their service, wherein they made them serve, was with rigour" (Exod. 1:13-14).

When God gave instructions for the construction of Solomon's Temple, no bricks were allowed. God wanted only materials from the earth that were unique, including stones. Each stone was different, yet when put together with others, they made something beautiful.

"Then David said, This is the house of the LORD God, and this is the altar of the burnt offering for Israel. And David commanded to gather together the strangers that were in the land of Israel; and he set masons to hew wrought stones to build the house of God.

Now, behold, in my trouble I have prepared for the house of the LORD an hundred thousand talents of gold, and a thousand thousand talents of silver; and of brass and iron without weight; for it is in abundance: timber also and stone have I prepared; and thou mayest add thereto" (1 Chron. 22:1-2, 14-15).

David set God's people free from the bondage of the Philistines using stones to defeat their hero, Goliath.

"And he took his staff in his hand, and chose him five smooth stones out of the brook, and put them in a shepherd's bag which he had, even in a scrip; and his sling was in his hand: and he drew near to the Philistine. And David put his hand in his bag, and took thence a stone, and slang it, and smote the Philistine in his forehead, that the stone sunk into his forehead; and he fell upon his face to the earth. So David prevailed over the Philistine with a sling and with a stone, and smote the Philistine, and slew him; but there was no sword in the hand of David. Therefore David ran, and stood upon the Philistine, and took his sword, and drew it out of the sheath thereof, and slew him, and cut off his head therewith. And when the Philistines saw their champion was dead, they fled" (1 Sam. 17:40, 49-51).

When God separated the people by confusing their language, it made it easier for people to show their differences. It was harder for man to communicate and thus unite in evil global plans that ignore the faith principles of God. God has made it so that the pride of different groups and nations restrict the pride of other groups and nations. God knows the potential of prideful men to design their own security system without trusting in God, our real source of supply.

It is a beautiful thing to see the different nations with their various languages, music, architectures, cuisines, climates, landscapes, scenery, markets, traditions and cultures. All of these various people and nations have been invited by Jesus to become a joint heir with him. God separated the nations so that people would have the best chance to enter into the kingdom of God. Each person is a unique "whosoever."

"For God so loved the world, that he gave his only begotten Son, that whosoever believeth in him should not perish, but have everlasting life. For God sent not his Son into the world to condemn the world; but that the world through him might be saved" (John 3:16-17).

"And they sung a new song, saying, Thou art worthy to take the book, and to open the seals thereof: for thou wast slain, and hast redeemed us to God by thy blood out of every kindred, and tongue, and people, and nation; And hast made us unto our God kings and priests: and we shall reign on the earth" (Rev. 5:9-10).

God is not stingy. He wants to share his abundant life with each one of us. There is plenty to go around. There is no shortage in heaven! There has never been a recession, depression, or global crisis in the kingdom of God. In heaven, there are whole cities and streets made of pure gold. As we trust God, we tap into abundance and an inexhaustible supply for every area of our lives.

"For ye have not received the spirit of bondage again to fear; but ye have received the Spirit of adoption, whereby we cry, Abba, Father. The Spirit itself beareth witness with our spirit, that we are the children of God: And if children, then heirs; heirs of God, and joint-heirs with Christ; if so be that we suffer with him, that we may be also glorified together" (Rom. 8:15-17).

"For the LORD God is a sun and shield: the LORD will give grace and glory: no good thing will he withhold from them that walk uprightly. O LORD of hosts, blessed is the man that trusteth in thee" (Ps. 84:11).

God separated the people into various nations because he doesn't want a global currency or a global language and certainly not a global government. God went out of his way to prevent a new world order or an open society without borders.

"Go to, let us go down, and there confound their language, that they may not understand one another's speech. So the LORD scattered them abroad from thence upon the face of all the earth: and they left off to build the city" (Gen. 11:7-8).

Whenever there is a global society, the potential for a global crisis is greater. Today, people try to create a global crisis in order to achieve evil plans that entail manifesting power over people, convincing them that they are "bricks" and not "stones." They create an illusion that the normal challenges of life are too big and too complicated, and only the brilliant leaders of government have the answers.

Sadly, through fear, many people give up the inheritance of their children and grandchildren in order to cling to government provision. It's the same thing that happened in the book of Genesis. They chose to make government their provider instead of God Almighty. If it weren't so tragic, it would be comical. If you listen to many politicians today as they talk about economic issues, it becomes apparent that they probably can't reconcile their own checkbooks.

Again, the devil's system of the world (Babylonian system) is an economic system based on fear. The primary principle is buying and selling. The system of the Kingdom of God is a system of love and is based on faith as "faith worketh by love." The primary principle is sowing and reaping.

The world system puts people in bondage through fear of not having enough money. The primary principle of buying and selling causes people to toil and "in the sweat of thy face shalt thou eat bread" (Gen. 3:19a). This is a cursed system. In the world system, you get ahead at the expense of someone else. You step on someone else to get to the top. God says that we're no longer to conform to the world but completely leave the world system and operate according to the principles of the kingdom of God. We can't serve two masters. I'm not saying that you should quit your job, but I am saying you should receive the revelation that God is your source of supply and not your job.

Abraham's part of his covenant with God was that he had to come out of his country and his kindred. In other words, he had to come out of the system he depended on and depend upon God to bless him so much that he could be a blessing to the whole world.

"Now the LORD had said unto Abram, Get thee out of thy country, and from thy kindred, and from thy father's house, unto a land that I will shew thee: And I will make of thee a great nation, and I will bless thee, and make thy name great; and thou shalt be a blessing: And I will bless them that bless thee, and curse him that curseth thee: and in thee shall all families of the earth be blessed" (Gen. 12:1-3).

This blessing is for us today as, through Christ, we become Abraham's seed. We are blessed to be a blessing. As we operate in kingdom principles, God prospers us so much that we can be a blessing to others. We are led by the Spirit of God to give where it is productive, and great good is achieved. That is exactly how capitalism works. Money goes where it is producing the most. It is a natural picture of a spiritual kingdom. The direct opposite of this kingdom principle is taking money from the producers and giving it to wasteful government programs or to those that have evil intentions.

A great example of this is Planned Parenthood. Remember, in the world system, you get ahead through the detriment of someone else. Planned Parenthood gets the vast amount of its revenue streams from the slaughter of innocent children. The government takes your hard-earned tax dollars and gives to this evil organization, thus making it easier for them to execute these heinous crimes.

The system of the kingdom of God causes us to prosper as we gather in the harvest from our seeds that we have sown. Christ has redeemed us from the curse. In the kingdom of God, we prosper as we bless others. We still may buy and sell, but we do it with integrity, trusting that God is faithful. As we operate in faith as we invest in the kingdom, we are blessed as finances move from the unproductive to the productive by the power of God. This will guarantee our success regardless of the economy, or who is in office, how high taxes are, how high the price of oil is, or how high food prices are. We don't have to be afraid, because God's principles always work.

"Every good gift and every perfect gift is from above, and cometh down from the Father of lights, with whom is no variableness, neither shadow of turning" (Jas. 1:17).

If our thinking lines up with the Kingdom of God, we believe God for the promised abundant life as we operate according to his principles that we were taught in Luke chapter 19. These principles are consistently revealed throughout the entire word of God. The abundant life means that we enjoy life and have it to the full until it overflows. Many Christians still operate according to the world system and walk in the bondage of fear, even if they are wealthy. They have a scarcity mentality. This world-conforming thought process causes them to act like the world and miss opportunities to sow or share what they have because of the fear of running out.

The only real security for tomorrow comes from what we give away today. Even the richest people in the world system walk in fear for what might happen tomorrow to cause them to lose what they have. That's why they have to take what belongs to others in an attempt to calm their fears. A lack of a sense of security drives them to make others into "bricks." This is the opposite of how God operates. God does not want each life to be the same as the next man but that each would receive and be blessed in a unique way according to how God has gifted him.

'Now there are diversities of gifts, but the same Spirit. And there are differences of administrations, but the same Lord. And there are diversities of operations, but it is the same God which worketh all in all. But the manifestation of the Spirit is given to every man to profit withal. For to one is given by the Spirit the word of wisdom; to another the word of knowledge by the same Spirit; To another faith by the same Spirit; to another the gifts of healing by the same Spirit; To another the working of miracles; to another prophecy; to another discerning of spirits; to another divers kinds of tongues; to another the interpretation of tongues: But all these worketh that one and the selfsame Spirit, dividing to every man severally as he will" (1 Cor. 12:4-11).

Remember, you are as unique as a stone and you are made to glorify God in a special way. No one else can do what you do. You are not a brick. In Jesus, you are a precious, beautiful, living stone.

"If so be ye have tasted that the Lord is gracious. To whom coming, as unto a living stone, disallowed indeed of men, but chosen of God, and precious, Ye also, as lively stones, are built up a spiritual house, an holy priesthood, to offer up spiritual sacrifices, acceptable to God by Jesus Christ" (1 Pet. 2:3-5).

CHAPTER SIX

GIVING TO GET

The Babylonian system of wealth distribution is based on taking from others to increase yourself. God's wealth distribution system is based on giving to others, and then you are increased. If God's wealth transfer plan is going to work, then we must *expect* to receive when we give. We always get what we expect. What we believe is where we end up.

"For as he thinketh in his heart, so is he" (Prov. 23:7a).

God wants his people to know that he is for them and not against them. God loves you and is interested in you and cares about what you care about. Those who love God are interested in what he is interested in and what he cares about. What does God care about? He cares about reaching the lost (those not in covenant with him) and he cares about his beloved (those in covenant with him). He wants everyone to be born again and to be part of his beloved.

"Beloved, I wish above all things that thou mayest prosper and be in health, even as thy soul prospereth" (3 John 2).

"And he said unto them, Go ye into all the world, and preach the gospel to every creature" (Mark 16:15).

"What man of you, having an hundred sheep, if he lose one of them, doth not leave the ninety and nine in the wilderness, and go after that which is lost, until he find it? And when he hath found it, he layeth it on his shoulders, rejoicing" (Luke 15:4-5).

"But the father said to his servants, Bring forth the best robe, and put it on him; and put a ring on his hand, and shoes on his feet: And bring hither the fatted calf, and kill it; and let us eat, and be merry: For this my son was dead, and is alive again; he was lost, and is found. And they began to be merry" (Luke 15:22-24).

God wants his beloved to prosper and be in health, not only because he loves us, but also because we are the ones who will be faithful and invest in the Kingdom of God. I have found that I can do more for the Kingdom of God with my health and resources than I can if I'm sick and broke.

God wants prosperity in the hands of those who care about his work and his interests, so we can do something about what he is concerned about, namely, reaching the lost and healing his beloved. To accomplish this, God gives his people power to gain wealth to establish his covenant. The covenant is accomplished through the giving principle and as we obey him in giving, God's reward system kicks in.

"But thou shalt remember the LORD thy God: for it is he that giveth thee power to get wealth, that he may establish his covenant which he sware unto thy fathers, as it is this day" (Deut. 8:18).

"But this I say, He which soweth sparingly shall reap also sparingly; and he which soweth bountifully shall reap also bountifully. Every man according as he purposeth in his heart, so let him give; not grudgingly, or of necessity: for God loveth a cheerful giver" (1 Cor. 9:6-7).

Every time I sow a seed into the kingdom of God, I do it cheerfully, and I decide what to give. Every time I "give" to the IRS, I do it grudgingly and out of necessity, and they decide how much I "give."

Excessive government controls over our life hinder the working of God's plan. Remember, it is in the environment of liberty that we can fully bless the nations of the world. We have to first be blessed to be a blessing. We need to get into the right mentality in order to walk in the fullness of the blessings of God. To get in the right mentality we need to learn to expect to receive when we give. We can accomplish this by studying the parable of the unjust steward in Luke chapter 16.

"And he said also unto his disciples, There was a certain rich man, which had a steward; and the same was accused unto him that he had wasted his goods. And he called him, and said unto him, How is it that I hear this of thee? Give an account of thy stewardship; for thou mayest be no longer steward. Then the steward said within himself, What shall I do? for my lord taketh away from me the stewardship: I cannot dig; to beg I am ashamed. I am resolved what to do, that, when I am put out of the stewardship, they may receive me into their houses. So he called every one of his lord's debtors unto him, and said unto the first, How much owest thou unto my lord? And he said, An hundred measures of oil. And he said unto him, Take thy bill, and sit down quickly, and write fifty. Then said he to another, And how much owest thou? And he said, An hundred measures of wheat. And he said unto him, Take thy bill, and write fourscore. And the lord commended the unjust steward, because he had done wisely: for the children of this world are in their generation wiser than the children of light" (Luke 16:1-8).

The unjust steward knew what he must do, and did it. He gave away what belonged to the rich man so that when (not if, but when) he's put out of the stewardship, he would be received into one of the rich man's debtors' houses. He wanted a place to go when he gets fired.

He definitely gave to get. He gave expecting to receive. Based on our natural minds, we think that verse 8 should say, "you gave away a lot of my money just so you'd have a place to go and because of that you are fired!" Yet, the rich man doesn't say that. In fact, the rich man commends the unjust steward.

"And the lord commended the unjust steward, because he had done wisely: for the children of this world are in their generation wiser than the children of light" (Luke 16:8a).

The steward knew a principle. He knew that what he gave away would come back to him to secure his personal future. The rich man also knew this principle. The rich man had a lot of wisdom. That's why he was so rich. He was pleased with the steward because he had learned how to be a success in life and bless the rich man in the process. That's the kind of steward he wanted.

Apparently, he not only kept the steward on the job, but probably gave him a raise. The rich man was pleased with the steward and said that he had done wisely. If he is wiser, he is worth more money.

Why would Jesus say that the children of this world are wiser than the children of light? In other words, he is saying that, in that generation, the world understands giving to get better than his people. They understand the concept of "you scratch my back and I'll scratch your back." They understand "let's work together," even if they use this principle for evil means like building the Tower of Babel. In the generation that will lead to the end-time wealth transfer, God's people will surpass the world in the use of this powerful kingdom principle of giving in order to receive.

The steward gave while expecting to receive. Jesus told his disciples that not only did the rich man commend the steward, but he also affirmed him by saying that he was wiser than the children of light. Why was he wiser? Because he gave believing—believing his giving was going to come back to him and salvage his future. He trusted upon the giving principle to salvage his future when he lost his permanent security of his job.

Who is the rich man in this parable, the one who let the steward know that he would be called to account for his stewardship, and thus caused the steward to lose his permanent security in his job? Let's look at verses 1 and 2 again.

"And he said also unto his disciples, There was a certain rich man, which had a steward; and the same was accused unto him that he had wasted his goods. And he called him, and said unto him, How is it that I hear this of thee? Give an account of thy stewardship; for thou mayest be no longer steward" (Luke 16:1-2).

God is the rich man and Adam is the steward. Adam was God's steward over the earth. God and Adam visited and fellowshipped every day, and Adam gave an account of himself. The earth belonged to God, but Adam was in charge. Even after Adam messed up, God came calling for his daily visit.

"And they heard the voice of the LORD God walking in the garden in the cool of the day: and Adam and his wife hid themselves from the presence of the LORD God amongst the trees of the garden. And the LORD God called unto Adam, and said unto him, Where art thou? And he said, I heard thy voice in the garden, and I was afraid, because I was naked; and I hid myself. And he said, Who told thee that thou wast naked? Hast thou eaten of the tree, whereof I commanded thee that thou shouldest not eat?" (Gen. 3:8-11).

Adam lost his position of steward, through non-compliance of God's directions, when he ate the forbidden fruit. God called Adam to give an account of his stewardship, and he had no answer. There was nothing he could do to redeem himself. God still loved Adam and wanted his fellowship, but he could not fellowship with Adam the way that he was. Adam couldn't fix the situation, so if God wanted our fellowship, he had to do something. Adam had no answer, so God himself reveals the answer.

"I am resolved what to do, that, when I am put out of the stewardship, they may receive me into their houses" (Luke 16:4).

God took his very best, his Word, and put him in the form of what he wanted to receive– man. Then he sowed him into the ground.

"Verily, verily, I say unto you, Except a corn of wheat fall into the ground and die, it abideth alone: but if it die, it bringeth forth much fruit" (John 12:24).

When the Father sowed Jesus, he didn't just want Jesus back. He sowed him to get us. We are the increase. The kind of harvest you want determines the kind of seed you sow. God must have had great confidence in the principle he put on the earth—that what you sow, you reap, and you also receive increase.

"Be not deceived; God is not mocked: for whatsoever a man soweth, that shall he also reap" (Gal. 6:7).

"Give, and it shall be given unto you; good measure, pressed down, and shaken together, and running over, shall men give into your bosom. For with the same measure that ye mete withal it shall be measured to you again" (Luke 6:38).

Let's examine the greatest gift that has ever been given.

"For God so loved the world, that he gave his only begotten Son, that whosoever believeth in him should not perish, but have everlasting life" (John 3:16).

Love motivated God to give, but he also gave for a desired result. The Father gave Jesus so he could have us. God gave expecting to receive back what he sowed with increase. He gave so that we might have everlasting life. Love is his motive, but giving is his method.

Love motivated God to give. He loved us and wanted our fellowship. He knew that to get what he wanted, he had to sow a seed. We should know the same thing. The love that motivated God produced or worked the faith to believe for the desired result. In this case, that you and I would have everlasting life.

"For in Jesus Christ neither circumcision availeth anything, nor uncircumcision; but faith which worketh by love" (Gal. 5:6).

If giving in order to receive is wrong, then God Almighty was wrong. What about the person who says, "I just want to give out of love and expect nothing back. I just want to please God." Where's

81

the faith in that? This may appear sweet and spiritual at first glance, but the Bible says that "without faith it is impossible to please him" (Heb. 11:6a). You see, it is not a choice of love or receiving. It's both or nothing, because faith works by love. The motive of love works the faith to receive the harvest with increase. Without love as your motive, you will fail in your faith to believe and receive the increase.

Did God's seed work? On the third day God's seed sprouted. Your seed, if you are expecting a harvest, will sprout too. No natural or spiritual force can stop a seed sown in faith. Jesus' body was laid in a tomb, covered by a great rock, sealed with Pilate's seal, and guarded by Pilate's soldiers.

"And when Joseph had taken the body, he wrapped it in a clean linen cloth, and laid it in his own new tomb, which he had hewn out in the rock: and he rolled a great stone to the door of the sepulchre, and departed" (Matt. 27:59-60).

"Command therefore that the sepulchre be made sure until the third day, lest his disciples come by night, and steal him away, and say unto the people, He is risen from the dead: so the last error shall be worse than the first. Pilate said unto them, Ye have a watch: go your way, make it as sure as ye can. So they went, and made the sepulchre sure, sealing the stone, and setting a watch" (Matt. 27:64-66).

They couldn't stop the resurrection of Jesus Christ, the Son of God. Did he come up by himself? No, there was increase. Graves opened up all over Jerusalem. He was the first fruits of them that sleep. God sowed a seed in faith and believed when he did he would receive a harvest with increase. He must have believed in his system to give his only begotten son over to it.

"And the graves were opened; and many bodies of the saints which slept arose, and came out of the graves after his resurrection, and went into the holy city, and appeared unto many" (Matt. 27: 52-53).

Jesus replaced Adam as the unjust steward. Adam didn't know what to do, but Jesus did, and the Father was well pleased. Adam, through sin, became an unjust steward. Jesus took his place as the second and last Adam.

"But now is Christ risen from the dead, and become the firstfruits of them that slept. For since by man came death, by man came also the resurrection of the dead. For as in Adam all die, even so in Christ shall all be made alive" (1 Cor. 15:20-22).

"So also is the resurrection of the dead. It is sown in corruption; it is raised in incorruption: It is sown in dishonour; it is raised in glory: it is sown in weakness; it is raised in power: It is sown a natural body; it is raised a spiritual body. There is a natural body, and there is a spiritual body. And so it is written, The first man Adam was made a living soul; the last Adam was made a quickening spirit. Howbeit that was not first which is spiritual, but that which is natural; and afterward that which is spiritual. The first man is of the earth, earthy: the second man is the Lord from heaven" (1 Cor. 15:42-47).

He was still called the unjust steward when he gave away the good things that belonged to the Father. Jesus, who was without sin, actually became the unjust steward by taking on the sins of the world.

"For he hath made him to be sin for us, who knew no sin; that we might be made the righteousness of God in him" (2 Cor. 5:21).

As the unjust steward, Jesus was resolved what to do. He gave varying degrees of discounts to the rich man's debtors and gave away the rich man's goods. He gave sight to the blind, health to those that were sick, the ability to walk to those with lame feet, courage to the discouraged, and he gave and he gave.

"How God anointed Jesus of Nazareth with the Holy Ghost and with power: who went about doing good, and healing all that were oppressed of the devil; for God was with him" (Acts: 10:38).

It worked. We love him, and his Father (the rich man) commended him.

"We love him, because he first loved us" (1 John 4:19).

"And Jesus, when he was baptized, went up straightway out of the water: and, lo, the heavens were opened unto him, and he saw the Spirit of God descending like a dove, and lighting upon him: And lo a voice from heaven, saying, This is my beloved Son, in whom I am well pleased" (Matt. 3:16-17).

"Then answered Peter, and said unto Jesus, Lord, it is good for us to be here: if thou wilt, let us make here three tabernacles; one for thee, and one for Moses, and one for Elias. While he yet spake, behold, a bright cloud overshadowed them: and behold a voice out of the cloud, which said, This is my beloved Son, in whom I am well pleased; hear ye him" (Matt. 17:4-5).

Jesus, as the unjust steward, called every one of the rich man's debtors, because no one could pay what was owed. Are we not all a debtor to the Father (the rich man)? Have we not all sinned and fallen short of the glory of God? Some of us may need bigger discounts than others, but none of us can pay what we owe. Thank God that Jesus understands and the Father approves of giving while expecting to receive.

"For all have sinned, and come short of the glory of God; Being justified freely by his grace through the redemption that is in Christ Jesus" (Rom. 3:23-24).

In fact, the Father was so pleased with Jesus that he didn't fire him for giving away all his goodness, but instead gave him a raise. He gave him the greatest raise that was ever given.

"Let this mind be in you, which was also in Christ Jesus: Who, being in the form of God, thought it not robbery to be equal with God: But made himself of no reputation, and took upon him the form of a servant, and was made in the likeness of men: And being found in fashion as a man, he humbled himself, and became obedient unto death, even the death of the cross. Wherefore God also hath highly exalted him, and given him a name which is above every name: That at the name of Jesus every knee should bow, of things in heaven, and things in earth, and things under the earth; And that every tongue should confess that Jesus Christ is Lord, to the glory of God the Father" (Phil. 2:5-11).

Jesus will let us share the fruits of his raise as we become joint heirs with him by grace through faith.

"For by grace are ye saved through faith; and that not of yourselves: it is the gift of God: Not of works, lest any man should boast" (Eph. 2:8-9).

God's system of sowing and reaping causes capital to go where it is the most productive. In the Kingdom of God, when you invest you expect to gain by trading or making increase. In other words, make a profit on your investment. This is not considered as something wrong or ungodly but as something that pleases God and results from godly wisdom.

"And the lord commended the unjust steward, because he had done wisely" (Luke 16:8a).

This notion of gaining increase or making a profit is placed in us by God. Even socialists want to make money when they make an investment. I've never heard one of them complain if their 401k goes up. If they really believed in their philosophy, they should want their 401k to go down or at least remain constant.

I have talked with several bankers who have over 100 years combined experience. None of them remembers any clients asking that posted interest to their accounts be removed. God places the desire for increase in us because we are made in the image of God, and God likes increase. In Luke 19, we see that he rewards his servants based on how much increase they generate. God wants you to desire a profit and to make a profit. God does not consider profits as evil. In fact, God considers a lack of profit or increase as evil.

"For the kingdom of heaven is as a man travelling into a far country, who called his own servants, and delivered unto them his goods. And unto one he gave five talents, to another two, and to another one; to every man according to his several ability; and straightway took his journey. Then he that had received the five talents went and traded with the same, and made them other five talents. And likewise he that had received two, he also gained other two. But he that had received one went and digged in the earth, and hid his lord's money. After a long time the lord of those servants cometh, and reckoneth with them. And so he that had received five talents came and brought other five talents, saying, Lord, thou deliveredst unto me five talents: behold, I have gained beside them five talents more. His lord said unto him, Well done, thou good and faithful servant: thou hast been faithful over a few things, I will make thee ruler over many things: enter thou into the joy of thy lord. He also that had received two talents came and said, Lord, thou deliveredst unto me two talents: behold, I have gained two other talents beside them. His lord said unto him, Well done, good and faithful servant; thou hast been faithful over a few things, I will make thee ruler over many things: enter thou into the joy of thy lord. Then he which had received the one talent came and said, Lord, I knew thee that thou art an hard man, reaping where thou hast not sown, and gathering where thou hast not strawed: And I was afraid, and went and hid thy talent in the earth: lo, there thou hast that is thine. His lord answered and said unto him, Thou wicked and slothful servant, thou knewest that I reap where I sowed not, and gather where I have not strawed: Thou oughtest therefore to have put my money to the exchangers, and then at my coming I should have received mine own with usury. Take therefore the talent from him, and give it unto him which hath ten talents. For unto every one that hath shall be given, and he shall have abundance: but from him that hath not shall be taken away even that which he hath. And cast ye the unprofitable servant into outer darkness: there shall be weeping and gnashing of teeth." (Matt. 25:14-30).

Those who made a profit were rewarded according to how much profit they produced, and the unprofitable servant was severely punished. There was weeping and gnashing of teeth! Socialism that produces laziness is displeasing to God and hurts people. It takes away people's dignity and self-respect. It makes them see themselves as just bricks. Capitalism, which causes people to be reward-motivated, pleases God and blesses people. It produces high self-esteem as people see themselves as unique as individual stones.

A socialist can't help others very much. A good capitalist has extra to help others, provides a good, helpful product at a good price for customers, and provides a good wage for employees to take care of their families. The higher the profits, the higher wages he can pay. You have to be blessed to be a blessing. I've never heard of a poor man or a bankrupt company offering a job. Abundance is the normal way of the kingdom of God.

God has made us to be reward motivated. Don't let the devil talk you out of your destiny with God. Let's learn some more about God's system of reward motivation to produce good on the earth.

CHAPTER SEVEN

GOD IS A REWARDER

If we want to please God, we have to produce fruit. That was God's first instruction to Adam. It is still his first instruction to us today, because he treats everyone the same and he never changes.

"Then Peter opened his mouth, and said, Of a truth I perceive that God is no respecter of persons" (Acts 10:34).

"For I am the LORD, I change not" (Mal. 3:6a).

God expects each one of us to produce fruit and bring forth increase. He gives each one of us equal opportunity, as he is not a respecter of persons.

"And God blessed them, and God said unto them, Be fruitful, and multiply, and replenish the earth, and subdue it: and have dominion over the fish of the sea, and over the fowl of the air, and over every living thing that moveth upon the earth" (Gen. 1:28).

Because God has given us a free will and God made each of us unique, it is evil to try to manipulate equal outcomes in people's lives. God does not guarantee equal outcomes, but he does give us equal opportunities to be blessed. We are blessed through trust in God. God has given us an incentive to obey through his promises of reward for obedience. Increased fruit, multiplication, and replenishment of the earth are manifested through his reward system. Doesn't a salesman produce more sales when paid on a commission basis as opposed to a flat salary regardless of the results?

"Every man shall receive his own reward according to his own labour" (1 Cor. 3:8b).

"Be ye strong therefore, and let not your hands be weak: for your work shall be rewarded" (2 Chron. 15:7)

God wants you to know that there are rewards waiting for you. We receive them by seeking first his kingdom (with its primary principle of sowing and reaping) and his righteousness. We seek God, we obey his laws, and we operate according to his principles. We seek God—not prosperity. Yet, we know by faith that we will prosper as we obey. Prosperity is, without fail, a by-product of obedience.

If you are butchering a cow to make steaks, there will always be material to make hot dogs. The hot dogs are merely a by-product of the process to make steaks. Prosperity is merely a by-product of the process of obedience to kingdom principles, because the primary principle is sowing and reaping.

Again, God wants you to know about his reward. You can't be motivated to seek him unless you know that he is a rewarder.

"But without faith it is impossible to please him: for he that cometh to God must believe that he is, and that he is a rewarder of them that diligently seek him" (Heb. 11:6).

God has a unique race for each of us to run. Each man's reward is based on his running *his own* race. There are no rewards for running someone else's race. The idea of trying to make many people run the same race originated from the pits of hell. It is evil, demonic, and straight from the devil himself. This destroys people. It keeps them from receiving their reward and keeps them from fulfilling their kingdom destiny. This notion is contrary to God's plan of love and is based on hate. The apostle Paul ran a race of love and finished his race for his reward.

"For though I be free from all men, yet have I made myself servant unto all, that I might gain the more. Know ye not that they which run in a race run all, but one receiveth the prize? So run, that ye may obtain. And every man that striveth for the mastery is temperate in all things. Now they do it to obtain a corruptible crown; but we an incorruptible. I therefore so run, not as uncertainly; so fight I, not as one that beateth the air: But I keep under my body, and bring it into subjection: lest that by any means, when I have preached to others, I myself should be a castaway" (1 Cor. 9:19, 24-27).

"I have fought a good fight, I have finished my course, I have kept the faith: Henceforth there is laid up for me a crown of righteousness, which the Lord, the righteous judge, shall give me at that day: and not to me only, but unto all them also that love his appearing" (2 Tim. 4:7-8).

The apostle Paul was reward motivated, and you should be too. Remember, we have to believe and expect our rewards. If you are not expecting rewards, then you have no faith in the promises of God, and without faith it is impossible to please him.

God wants us to be reward motivated. If we are, we are functioning the way God intended. God likes it when we believe him and expect him to keep his word. Throughout the Bible, God says that if you do A, I'll reward you with B. What is the best way to show him you believe him? Is it by saying, "Lord, I believe you," or is it simply to do A because you expect B?

The apostle Paul was in good company of many great people of God who were reward motivated. Let's look at David, for example. With help from God, David pulled off one of the greatest victories in the Bible when he defeated Goliath. Did you know that without the promise of reward, David would have never even faced Goliath? David was afraid like everyone else when he first saw and heard Goliath.

David, sent by his father Jesse, went to the men of Israel's camp at the valley of Elah to bring food to his brothers and to his brothers' captain. He found his brothers, and as he talked with them, Goliath came out and issued his challenge to Israel once again.

"And as he talked with them, behold, there came up the champion, the Philistine of Gath, Goliath by name, out of the armies of the Philistines, and spake according to the same words: and David heard them. And all the men of Israel, when they saw the man, fled from him, and were sore afraid" (1 Sam. 17:23-24).

David heard the words. The Bible said that all the men of Israel, which would include David, fled and were very afraid. What happened to cause David to go from a place of fear to the place of wanting to challenge Goliath? It was the promised reward. After thinking about the reward, David recalled the time he defeated the lion and the bear; he then determined that God could bring him to victory.

"And the men of Israel said, Have ye seen this man that is come up? surely to defy Israel is he come up: and it shall be, that the man who killeth him, the king will enrich him with great riches, and will give him his daughter, and make his father's house free in Israel" (1 Sam. 17:25).

The thing that triggered the faith David needed to fulfill his kingdom destiny was the promise of reward. The reason the promise of reward didn't produce the same kind of faith in the other men is because they weren't as convinced about the faithfulness of God as David was. God's faithfulness had already been proven to David with victories over the lion and the bear. David sought out Saul for a chance at the reward.

"Thy servant slew both the lion and the bear: and this uncircumcised Philistine shall be as one of them, seeing he hath defied the armies of the living God. David said moreover, The LORD that delivered me out of the paw of the lion, and out of the paw of the bear, he will deliver me out of the hand of this Philistine. And Saul said unto David, Go, and the LORD be with thee. And Saul armed David with his armour, and he put an helmet of brass upon his head; also he armed him with a coat of mail. And David girded his sword upon his armour, and he assayed to go; for he had not proved it. And David said unto Saul, I cannot go with these; for I have not proved them. And David put them off him. And he took his staff in his hand, and chose him five smooth stones out of the brook, and put them in a shepherd's bag which he had, even in a scrip; and his sling was in his hand: and he drew near to the Philistine" (1 Sam. 17:36-40).

David had to run his own race. He couldn't be like Saul and try to run Saul's race. If he would have taken on Goliath with Saul's armor, he would have been defeated. He ran the race set before *him* and thereby fulfilled his kingdom destiny. David was reward motivated.

Moses was also reward motivated. He understood that God's reward is better than man's reward. In fact, the least of God's reward is greater than man's best reward.

"By faith Moses, when he was come to years, refused to be called the son of Pharaoh's daughter; Choosing rather to suffer affliction with the people of God, than to enjoy the pleasures of sin for a season; Esteeming the reproach of Christ greater riches than the treasures in Egypt: for he had respect unto the recompence of the reward. By faith he forsook Egypt, not fearing the wrath of the king: for he endured, as seeing him who is invisible" (Heb. 11:24-27).

Now you see why God loves for us to believe for his rewards. Like Moses, we must keep our eyes on the unseen God as we believe in the promises of God. That's what faith is. You don't go by what you see and hear, you judge by the word of God. Anyone can go by what they see and hear in the natural. Serving God is not about a bunch of impossible rules. He's looking for someone to believe him. Our heavenly Father wants us to operate like Jesus and judge by the word of God only. As we do this, the wicked will get their just rewards.

"And there shall come forth a rod out of the stem of Jesse, and a Branch shall grow out of his roots: And the spirit of the LORD shall rest upon him, the spirit of wisdom and understanding, the spirit of counsel and might, the spirit of knowledge and of the fear of the LORD; And shall make him of quick understanding in the fear of the LORD: and he shall not judge after the sight of his eyes, neither reprove after the hearing of his ears: But with righteousness shall he judge the poor, and reprove with equity for the meek of the earth: and he shall smite the earth with the rod of his mouth, and with the breath of his lips shall he slay the wicked" (Isa. 11:1-4).

In the previous chapter, we established that if giving and expecting to receive back with increase is wrong, then our heavenly Father is wrong. Of course, he is never wrong. In this chapter we will establish that if being reward motivated is wrong, then Jesus was wrong. Of course, he was not wrong. If you are too righteous to be reward motivated, then your righteousness must exceed that of Jesus Christ, the Lamb of God without spot or blemish. Jesus was reward motivated.

"Wherefore seeing we also are compassed about with so great a cloud of witnesses, let us lay aside every weight, and the sin which doth so easily beset us, and let us run with patience the race that is set before us, Looking unto Jesus the author and finisher of our faith; who for the joy that was set before him endured the cross, despising the shame, and is set down at the right hand of the throne of God" (Heb. 12:1-2).

Jesus endured the cross and the shame of taking on all the sins of all time in exchange for the reward he wanted. The joy that was set before him was that you and I and every person would have the opportunity to be saved, healed, delivered, redeemed, and blessed. If being reward motivated is wrong, then Jesus was wrong.

Since we are supposed to be imitators of Christ, Jesus wants us to be reward motivated. He wants us to know that we don't have to wait until the sweet by and by to receive our rewards. We can receive most of our rewards while we are still on the earth. They come by the giving principle manifesting from reaping with increase from what we have sown. We don't have to wait until we are in heaven. We can receive them a hundred fold *now in this time.*

"Then Peter began to say unto him, Lo, we have left all, and have followed thee. And Jesus answered and said, Verily I say unto you, There is no man that hath left house, or brethren, or sisters, or father, or mother, or wife, or children, or lands, for my sake, and the gospel's, But he shall receive an hundredfold now in this time, houses, and brethren, and sisters, and mothers, and children, and lands, with persecutions; and in the world to come eternal life" (Mark 10:28-30).

If you reject a reward from God, then, through self-righteousness, you have rejected God himself. God is our reward and in him is everything good that we could ever need or want. If we receive a reward from God, we are receiving God himself, for he told Abraham that he was our reward. That's why Jesus said to seek first the kingdom and then all the other things would be added to us. When we seek rewards from God, we are seeking God and his kingdom.

"After these things the word of the LORD came unto Abram in a vision, saying, Fear not, Abram: I am thy shield, and thy exceeding great reward" (Gen. 15:1)

"But seek ye first the kingdom of God, and his righteousness; and all these things shall be added unto you" (Matt. 6:33).

"This then is the message which we have heard of him, and declare unto you, that God is light, and in him is no darkness at all" (1 John 1:5).

The rewards of God will be manifested for the righteous and for the wicked. Everyone will be rewarded for the fruits they produce.

"Say ye to the righteous, that it shall be well with him: for they shall eat the fruit of their doings. Woe unto the wicked! it shall be ill with him: for the reward of his hands shall be given him" (Isa. 3:10-11).

Rewards from God are not just an Old Testament thing or just a New Testament thing. It's all through the Bible, because it is a God thing. There are some wonderful rewards that we will have to wait for his coming to receive. Jesus is so excited to give them to us that he isn't willing to wait an additional "twinkling of an eye" to give them to us. When he returns, he is bringing them with him.

"Behold, the LORD hath proclaimed unto the end of the world, Say ye to the daughter of Zion, Behold, thy salvation cometh; behold, his reward is with him, and his work before him" (Isa. 62:11).

"And, behold, I come quickly; and my reward is with me, to give every man according as his work shall be. I am Alpha and Omega, the beginning and the end, the first and the last" (Rev. 22:12-13).

The rewards of God are greatly to be sought after because God is our reward. They come to us as we seek him and give to and help others. In a capitalistic system, people succeed when they can help and solve problems for others. Don't seek the rewards from man in a low-living, evil system of the devil called socialism.

We should want to go after God and his rewards with all our heart and all our might in an environment that gives us the liberty to do that. It is called the pursuit of happiness as we pursuit our kingdom destiny. If we do, then one day we will receive even greater rewards than those we experienced on earth. It will be beyond what we can dream.

"For since the beginning of the world men have not heard, nor perceived by the ear, neither hath the eye seen, O God, beside thee, what he hath prepared for him that waiteth for him" (Isa. 64:4).

"But as it is written, Eye hath not seen, nor ear heard, neither have entered into the heart of man, the things which God hath prepared for them that love him" (1 Cor. 2:9).

CHAPTER EIGHT

ONE NATION UNDER GOD

In the book of Genesis, God issues a challenge and offers an opportunity for some nation or people to accept. What is the challenge? It is a godly assignment to care for Abraham and his seed. Since God knows the future, he knew that it would be important to rise up a nation to help the chosen nation (and thus the people of Israel) at a specific time in history.

"And I will bless them that bless thee, and curse him that curseth thee: and in thee shall all families of the earth be blessed" (Gen. 12:3).

In the fifteenth century, Spain became known as the Second Zion. Throughout the world, no nation had a higher Jewish population than Spain. In 1492, King Ferdinand of Spain issued a decree that the Jewish people would no longer be welcome on Spanish soil.[1] During that same year, King Ferdinand and Queen Isabella approved the funding of Christopher Columbus' expedition to India. Instead of discovering a better route to India, Columbus discovered the Americas. The mainland that is now the United States of America was claimed for Spain.

I believe that the fact that such a renowned navigator as Columbus landed in America instead of India was God ordained and not merely a coincidence. This newly discovered land now known as the United States of America would become the next home away from home for the Jewish people.

Since no nation existed that was willing to accept the opportunity from God to bless Israel, God had to create a new nation. That nation would have to lay its foundation on the Word of God and have godly principles and personal liberty embedded in its government. Its founders would have to be godly men who were willing to be led by the Spirit of God to form the new nation. It would be a nation that would grow mighty because of its use of godly principles. It would have to promote such an environment of liberty that its free enterprise system would cause the nation to grow to such might and power that it would easily be recognized as the leading, most prosperous and influential nation on earth.

The United States became such a nation because our founding fathers obeyed God and formed this republic based on the Word and Spirit of God. They created a nation that was one nation, under God, indivisible, with liberty and justice for all. Because of the great influence of the United States, when the United States of America recognized the nation of Israel in 1948, virtually all of the rest of the world followed and did the same. This was the plan of God.

"That then the LORD thy God will turn thy captivity, and have compassion upon thee, and will return and gather thee from all the nations, whither the LORD thy God hath scattered thee. And the LORD thy God will bring thee into the land which thy fathers possessed, and thou shalt possess it; and he will do thee good, and multiply thee above thy fathers" (Deut. 30:3, 5).

"Therefore, behold, the days come, saith the LORD, that it shall no more be said, The LORD liveth, that brought up the children of

Israel out of the land of Egypt; But, The LORD liveth, that brought up the children of Israel from the land of the north, and from all the lands whither he had driven them: and I will bring them again into their land that I gave unto their fathers" (Jer. 16:14-15).

On midnight May 14, 1948, (Jerusalem time) the Provisional Government of Israel proclaimed a new State of Israel. Eleven minutes later, The United States, in the person of President Harry S. Truman, announced its recognition of the new nation on May 15, 1948. Five Arab armies (Egypt, Syria, Transjordan, Lebanon and Iraq) immediately invaded Israel on the same day it gained its independence. Few people gave the new country any chance of survival against such a combined force. The intentions of the attackers were declared by Azzam Pasha, Secretary-General of the Arab League: "This will be a war of extermination and a momentous massacre which will be spoken of like the Mongolian massacres and the Crusades."[2]

The Arab war to destroy Israel failed. Indeed, because of their aggression, the Arabs wound up with less territory than they would have had if they had accepted the U.N. partition. Israel received spoil once again. The Arab countries signed armistice agreements with Israel in 1949, starting with Egypt (February 24), followed by Lebanon (March 23), Jordan (April 3), and Syria (July 20). Iraq was the only country that did not sign an agreement with Israel, choosing instead to withdraw its troops and hand over its sector to Jordan's Arab Legion.[3] Once again, my advice to Arab nations is this: Don't mess with Israel. You cannot catch them off guard with a surprise attack.

"Behold, he that keepeth Israel shall neither slumber nor sleep" (Ps. 121:4).

The United States of America has been given an assignment from God to sponsor, support, and be a friend to Israel. Since the new State of Israel was established in 1948, every president of the United States has maintained that relationship and commitment to Israel. President Barack Obama (in office at the time of this writing) seems shaky on his commitment. He appears to be on the precipice of making us an enemy of Israel. I pray he gets the revelation that the enemies of Israel are the enemies of the God and the friends of Israel are the friends of God.

"And I will bless them that bless thee, and curse him that curseth thee: and in thee shall all families of the earth be blessed" (Gen. 12:3).

"For this is the covenant that I will make with the house of Israel after those days, saith the Lord; I will put my laws into their mind, and write them in their hearts: and I will be to them a God, and they shall be to me a people" (Heb. 8:10).

"And the LORD thy God will put all these curses upon thine enemies, and on them that hate thee, which persecuted thee" (Deut. 30:7).

"They have said, Come, and let us cut them off from being a nation; that the name of Israel may be no more in remembrance. For they have consulted together with one consent: they are confederate against thee: Who said, Let us take to ourselves the houses of God in possession. O my God, make them like a wheel; as the stubble before the wind. As the fire burneth a wood, and as the flame setteth the mountains on fire; So persecute them with thy tempest, and make them afraid with thy storm. Fill their faces with shame; that they may seek thy name, O LORD. Let them be confounded and troubled for ever; yea, let them be put to shame, and perish: That men may know that thou, whose name alone is JEHOVAH, art the most high over all the earth" (Ps. 83:4-5, 12-18).

The United States has been given another assignment from God. It is to prosper in the environment of liberty from a government of the people, by the people, and for the people. In so doing, we operate with a rewards mentality like that used in the government of God. Coupling that with the ensuing, resulting great prosperity, we give generously to get the gospel out all over the world.

The United States gives far more money for the support of the gospel than the rest of the world combined. Each year, the giving from our private citizens pays for nearly 90 percent of the total cost of missionary evangelism to the rest of the world.[4] Our prosperity and giving spirit is to be an example for the whole world.

We do not have to be ashamed of our prosperity. The American free-enterprise system was given to us by God. There is no need for an "apology tour." The United States of America has been a blessing to every country in the world. We are fulfilling our kingdom destiny to be blessed to be a blessing. Those who are trying to overload and destroy our financial system are evil and full of greed. The very thing that they accuse others of is the thing that they are chiefly guilty of.

The government of the United States is founded upon liberty brought forth by the Spirit of God. Using faithful men, God fashioned a natural law within a natural government as a picture of his perfect law of liberty, the Word of God. Knowing that not all men would accept him, in his mercy God gave us a government with checks and balances so that even unredeemed men could experience a taste of liberty on the earth. This was necessary for the United States to fulfill its godly assignment. This earthly government was a natural picture of the liberty we receive in Christ. When worked in conjunction with godly principles, it produces good works and the gospel is promoted with its good rewards. It helps us be blessed to be a blessing.

"Stand fast therefore in the liberty wherewith Christ hath made us free, and be not entangled again with the yoke of bondage. For, brethren, ye have been called unto liberty; only use not liberty for an occasion to the flesh, but by love serve one another" (Gal. 5:1, 13).

"But whoso looketh into the perfect law of liberty, and continueth therein, he being not a forgetful hearer, but a doer of the work, this man shall be blessed in his deed" (Jas. 1:25).

The foundation of our government in the United States is the Holy Spirit and the Word of God. During the founding era (1760-1805), the Bible was cited in 34 percent of notable quotations from our founding fathers.[5] Did you know that all fifty-five signers of the Declaration of Independence believed in the Bible as the divine truth, believed in the God of Scripture, and his personal intervention in our lives? Did you know that fifty-two of the fifty-five signers were deeply committed Christians? Immediately after creating the Declaration of Independence, the Continental Congress formed the American Bible Society and voted to purchase and import 20,000 copies of Scripture for the people of this new nation.[6]

If you doubt that our government was based on the Word of God, then consider these quotes from our founding fathers.

"The general principles on which the fathers achieved independence were ... the general principles of Christianity." John Adams

"It cannot be emphasized too strongly or too often that this great nation was founded not by religionists, but by Christians; not on religion, but on the Gospel of Jesus Christ. For that reason alone, people of other faiths have been afforded freedom of worship here." Patrick Henry

"The highest glory of the American Revolution was this: it connected in one indissoluble bond the principles of civil government with the principles of Christianity." John Quincy Adams

"We have staked the whole future of our new nation, not upon the power of government; far from it. We have staked the future of all political constitutions upon the capacity of each of ourselves to govern ourselves according to the moral principles of the Ten Commandments." James Madison

"Providence has given to our people the choice of their rulers and it is the duty as well as the privilege and interest of our Christian Nation to select and prefer Christians for their rulers." John Jay

"No people can be bound to acknowledge and adore the invisible hand which conducts the affairs of men more than the people of the United States....We ought to be no less persuaded that the propitious smiles of heaven can never be expected on a nation which disregards the eternal rules of order and right which heaven itself ordained." George Washington

The principles that established the government of the United States of America were principles found in the Word of God. We will examine the major principles found in the Declaration of Independence, the Constitution, and the Bill of Rights. We will then see where these principles are declared in the Bible. This process will reveal that a biblically based form of government must give individuals a great deal of personal liberty with little government intervention. There is a role for government, but its role should be kept to a minimum.

Both the Bible and the First, Second, Ninth, and Tenth Amendments embrace the importance of governing self and family as the first level of governance. The opposite of that, global governance, is an abomination to God as revealed in Genesis chapter 11 and explained in chapter 5 of this book.

"Moreover if thy brother shall trespass against thee, go and tell him his fault between thee and him alone: if he shall hear thee, thou hast gained thy brother. But if he will not hear thee, then take with thee one or two more, that in the mouth of two or three witnesses every word may be established. And if he shall neglect to hear them, tell it unto the church: but if he neglect to hear the church, let him be unto thee as an heathen man and a publican" (Matt. 18:15-18).

Our government was set up with three equal branches of government. We should be careful to maintain the checks and balances that these three independent branches can accomplish. When one or more of any of these branches are diminished, the result is loss of liberty. For example, if a president encroaches on the legislative branch by effectively making his own laws through edict or regulations, then the citizens suffer loss of freedoms. When this happens, as it has during the time of Obama-appointee

Cass Sunstein's term as Regulation Czar, it makes one branch of government appear more equal than the others. Thus, laws are made without the people being represented. The judicial, legislative, and executive branches of government are found in the Book of Isaiah.

"For the LORD is our judge, the LORD is our lawgiver, the LORD is our king; he will save us" (Isa. 33:22).

We were given these branches of government for checks and balances because our founding fathers were well versed in Christianity and knew that all men were sinners.

"For all have sinned, and come short of the glory of God; Being justified freely by his grace through the redemption that is in Christ Jesus" (Rom. 3:23-24).

The founders gave us property rights as established in the kingdom of God. They put these property rights in the Bill of Rights in the Fifth Amendment so that no property can be taken away without due process or without just compensation.

"Thou shalt not steal" (Exod. 20:15).

"Thou shalt not covet thy neighbour's house, thou shalt not covet thy neighbour's wife, nor his manservant, nor his maidservant, nor his ox, nor his ass, nor any thing that is thy neighbour's" (Exod. 20:17).

In other words, what God is saying is: Thou shalt have no socialism or Marxism. There are many other constitutional concepts based on the Word, such as liberty and free enterprise.

"If the Son therefore shall make you free, ye shall be free indeed" (John 8:36).

"Stand fast therefore in the liberty wherewith Christ hath made us free, and be not entangled again with the yoke of bondage" (Gal. 5:1).

"For so is the will of God, that with well doing ye may put to silence the ignorance of foolish men: As free, and not using your liberty for a cloke of maliciousness, but as the servants of God" (1 Pet. 2:15-16).

Another biblical principle included in the work of our founders is the truth that all men are created equal, as found in the Declaration of Independence. Their belief in the God of the Bible was so strong that to them, this principle was "self evident." It was self evident that all men were created equal and given certain rights that come from God and God alone. These rights do not come from government. These rights are life, liberty, and the pursuit of happiness. Those words are sweet to my eyes and to my ears. God has truly created all men equal and given us all the opportunity to receive a great inheritance.

"Then Peter opened his mouth, and said, Of a truth I perceive that God is no respecter of persons" (Acts 10:34).

"And hath made of one blood all nations of men for to dwell on all the face of the earth, and hath determined the times before appointed, and the bounds of their habitation; That they should seek the Lord, if haply they might feel after him, and find him, though he be not far from every one of us" (Acts 17:26-27).

"There is neither Jew nor Greek, there is neither bond nor free, there is neither male nor female: for ye are all one in Christ Jesus" (Gal. 3:28).

"He that spared not his own Son, but delivered him up for us all, how shall he not with him also freely give us all things?" (Rom. 8:32).

CHAPTER NINE

CAPITALISM, SOCIALISM, MARXISM, AND SOCIAL JUSTICE

Let's define these various philosophies of government so that we can properly compare and contrast them beginning with biblical capitalism. What is it? Capitalism is based primarily on the rule of law. This was imparted into our American government by God Almighty. The rule of law originated with the Hebrews and the Ten Commandments. In our US Constitution, there are specifically identified powers of the federal government. All powers not specifically enumerated as federal powers are reserved for the states.

American capitalism is also defined by the belief that God has given to mankind certain unalienable rights, including life, liberty, and the pursuit of happiness. The Bill of Rights tells us that we have the right of free speech, the right to bear arms, and other rights. (Healthcare, collective bargaining, and goods and services are not rights.) American capitalism includes the notion that there are biblical, unchanging moral values that protect the innocent. For example, it is still wrong to murder a child even if a majority thinks that it is a right.

With capitalism, there is equal treatment for all under the law because all men are created equal. There are property rights so that theft is against the law. The government has a responsibility to prosecute those who steal, and certainly should not participate in theft of the property of its citizens. In capitalism, there is free enterprise without government intervention unless it is to enforce the rule of law. The only biblical role of government is to administer justice, prevent evil, and punish evil so the rest of society can live in peace.

"Let every soul be subject unto the higher powers. For there is no power but of God: the powers that be are ordained of God. Whosoever therefore resisteth the power, resisteth the ordinance of God: and they that resist shall receive to themselves damnation. For rulers are not a terror to good works, but to the evil. Wilt thou then not be afraid of the power? do that which is good, and thou shalt have praise of the same: For he is the minister of God to thee for good. But if thou do that which is evil, be afraid; for he beareth not the sword in vain: for he is the minister of God, a revenger to execute wrath upon him that doeth evil. Wherefore ye must needs be subject, not only for wrath, but also for conscience sake. For for this cause pay ye tribute also: for they are God's ministers, attending continually upon this very thing. Render therefore to all their dues: tribute to whom tribute is due; custom to whom custom; fear to whom fear; honour to whom honour" (Rom. 13:1-7)

"Submit yourselves to every ordinance of man for the Lord's sake: whether it be to the king, as supreme; Or unto governors, as unto them that are sent by him for the punishment of evildoers, and for the praise of them that do well. For so is the will of God, that with well doing ye may put to silence the ignorance of foolish men: As free, and not using your liberty for a cloke of maliciousness, but as the servants of God. Honour all men. Love the brotherhood. Fear God. Honour the king" (1 Pet. 2:13-17).

Government, for the most part, should be hands-off and encourage free enterprise, not favor certain enterprises over others (such as subsidizing 'green energy' companies). Government should not bail out companies just because they are dying or failing. In capitalism, money goes where it is producing the most (see Luke 19:24). All products have a life cycle. For instance, should the U.S. government have bailed out and continued to subsidize slide rule manufacturers and buggy whip manufacturers? Hardly.

Capitalism, like Christianity, places a premium on self-government. If we can govern ourselves to obey God, do what is right, and help others, we should have great liberty. Our founders, as godly men, embraced this biblical principle.

"Now the Lord is that Spirit: and where the Spirit of the Lord is, there is liberty" (2 Cor. 3:17).

The liberty to serve God was so desired by our founders that they put the following Scripture from Leviticus 25:10 on the Liberty Bell. "Proclaim liberty throughout all the land unto all the inhabitants thereof."

Socialism is very similar to communism as both deny property rights. In a socialistic or communist government, the government controls all assets and the government can mandate certain activities. Marxism attempts to establish a classless society by using the power of the state to take money from some groups of citizens and give it to other groups. All of these are evil and unscriptural. God cannot bless stealing.

"The thief cometh not, but for to steal, and to kill, and to destroy: I am come that they might have life, and that they might have it more abundantly" (John 10:10).

Marxism has of late resurfaced with a new name, a name that is more palatable to the uninformed. They now call it social justice. Doesn't that sound great? But there is no justice in this modern term being used by Marxists to collapse the economy of the United States. Beware of those talking about social justice, especially those in the pulpit. Child of God, run from churches where this evil concept is taught. It is unscriptural, and it is meant to destroy the United States and Israel.

From now on, we will use the term "social justice" to encompass all of the legalized theft philosophies such as socialism, communism, Marxism, and liberation theology. Liberation theology extols the virtues of forced wealth redistribution and injects theology into the concept of social justice. Liberation theology will leave people without Christ and destined to be in torment for all eternity, as its basic tenet is collective salvation and not individual salvation. In this philosophy, to obtain collective salvation, people must redistribute wealth "fairly" among the collective group. This is the "salvation" Barack Obama received through his pastor of twenty years, Jeremiah Wright. On several occasions, our current president has stated that his individual salvation is based on the collective salvation of everyone.

President Obama also stated that individual salvation is based on collective salvation in his August 9, 1995, interview with Bill Thompson about his book *Dreams From My Father.* He made the same statement at the Campus Progress Conference on July 12, 2006, at Northwestern University on October 24, 2006, at Southern New Hampshire University on May 19, 2007, at Wesleyan University on May 25, 2008, and on many other occasions including those at Knox College, Xavier University, and the University of Chicago School of Medicine.[1] Liberation theology calls for political liberation rather than spiritual salvation. This theology is erroneous, as each one of us must stand alone before God.

"I the LORD search the heart, I try the reins, even to give every man according to his ways, and according to the fruit of his doings" (Jer. 17:10).

"For we must all appear before the judgment seat of Christ; that every one may receive the things done in his body, according to that he hath done, whether it be good or bad" (2 Cor. 5:10).

"For the Son of man shall come in the glory of his Father with his angels; and then he shall reward every man according to his works" (Matt. 16:27).

"And before him shall be gathered all nations: and he shall separate them one from another, as a shepherd divideth his sheep from the goats: And he shall set the sheep on his right hand, but the goats on the left" (Matt. 25:32)

Today, it is sometimes difficult to know what people mean when they talk about social justice. Post-modern social justice is a simple concept that can be clearly stated as follows:

Government (the ruling elite) may decide at any time to redistribute wealth and assets to manufacture equality of outcome to its citizens (the common people). The elites decide how much of the pie is available for the common folk. This is evil no matter how good the intentions some of the proponents may have.

In essence, social justice is just a modern version of the Robin Hood story. Steal from the rich and give to the poor. In the Robin

Hood story, it was true that King John, who had usurped the throne from the rightful King Richard, gathered his wealth through exploitation and oppression of the people with excessive taxes and regulations. Note that the government oppressed the people, not capitalists.

Marxists and social justice advocates labor under a mistaken premise that rich capitalists have acquired all of their wealth through the oppression of the poor. To the contrary, a good capitalist gathers increase because he has many happy employees and satisfied customers. Good capitalists bless people; they don't oppress people. The bigger the government gets the more it oppresses people. Those that advocate social justice need to examine their model. They are trying to save people from King John *but they are King John.* They try to build government, which brings oppression to the people, and oppression has Satan at its roots.

"How God anointed Jesus of Nazareth with the Holy Ghost and with power: who went about doing good, and healing all that were oppressed of the devil; for God was with him" (Acts 10:38).

Some people, especially those who champion social justice and liberation theology, think that they are smarter than God is. They think they know what is right better than God does. They are fools, and they are helping to destroy peoples' lives.

"He is the Rock, his work is perfect: for all his ways are judgment: a God of truth and without iniquity, just and right is he" (Deut. 32:4).

Excessive, progressively expanded government (beyond the scope of the Constitution) has oppressed all levels of our society, including Christians. This "nanny state" mentality has affected the thinking, to various degrees, of many Christians. The economic oppression of high taxes plus the mental oppression from worldly thought patterns have hindered the church from doing what it is supposed to do and that which the government cannot do.

True social justice (not Marxism) is accomplished through obedience to God's Word. Christians should have compassion and take care of those who cannot take care of themselves.

"Thou shalt not pervert the judgment of the stranger, nor of the fatherless; nor take a widow's raiment to pledge: But thou shalt remember that thou wast a bondman in Egypt, and the LORD thy God redeemed thee thence: therefore I command thee to do this thing. When thou cuttest down thine harvest in thy field, and hast forgot a sheaf in the field, thou shalt not go again to fetch it: it shall be for the stranger, for the fatherless, and for the widow: that the LORD thy God may bless thee in all the work of thine hands. When thou beatest thine olive tree, thou shalt not go over the boughs again: it shall be for the stranger, for the fatherless, and for the widow. When thou gatherest the grapes of thy vineyard, thou shalt not glean it afterward: it shall be for the stranger, for the fatherless, and for the widow" (Deut. 24:14-21).

God tells us plainly that we have a moral obligation to take care of those less fortunate than we are. We should do it out of love and out of a desire to obey God.

"Then shall the righteous answer him, saying, Lord, when saw we thee an hungred, and fed thee? or thirsty, and gave thee drink? When saw we thee a stranger, and took thee in? or naked, and clothed thee? Or when saw we thee sick, or in prison, and came unto thee? And the King shall answer and say unto them, Verily I say unto you, Inasmuch as ye have done it unto one of the least of these my brethren, ye have done it unto me" (Matt. 25:37-40).

"Pure religion and undefiled before God and the Father is this, to visit the fatherless and widows in their affliction, and to keep himself unspotted from the world" (Jas. 1:27).

We do these things because we want to please God and because as born again believers "the love of God is shed abroad in our hearts by the Holy Ghost which is given unto us" (Rom. 5:5b).

Which method is the quickest and most efficient method of getting help to someone in need, the local church, or a bunch of bureaucrats on far off Capitol Hill? People need more than just physical help; they need the love of God along with instruction and encouragement from the Word.

I will give you an example. Suppose a man stops by Words of Life Church in Humble, Texas. He says he is down and out and flat broke. He is driving back to where he has family and a new job waiting for him. He is low on gas, and he doesn't have enough to make it where his family lives. He certainly doesn't have time to sign up for a government program. Even if that were possible, the government does a terrible job of determining who is lying and who really needs help. They approve virtually every request, thus wasting money and perpetuating a growing dependence on government.

The pastor, who greets the traveler and listens to his story, is a man of God who, by the Holy Ghost, can discern the intent of the stranger's heart. The pastor, prompted by the Spirit of God, has the man follow him to a nearby convenience store that includes gas pumps. As the man goes into the restroom to clean up, the pastor fills up the stranger's car with gas and buys him a sandwich with chips and a drink. He gives the man $60.00 to make sure he can buy more gas, thereby insuring he can reach his destination without running out.

The stranger is so touched and grateful that he is willing to listen to anything the pastor has to say. They talk for a few minutes, and the pastor relays to the stranger God's simple plan of salvation. The stranger responds and asks Jesus to come into his heart and be his Lord and Savior. The pastor prays for him, blesses him in his new job, and sends the stranger on his way. The pastor's parting remarks let the stranger know that he is no longer a stranger to him, but now a brother in Christ. He tells him that even if he never sees him again on earth, one day they will see each other in heaven. All this takes place in less than thirty minutes.

Can government do that? Of course, they cannot. Even if they could respond that fast, it would probably be a wrong response. They could not minister under the anointing, as government officials are afraid to even mention God. A Marxist or social justice type government doesn't even believe in the existence of God. Marxists think that government is God and should replace what God does with what they do. Not only can government not do what God does, it can't even do what man can do through private enterprise. If you absolutely must have a package somewhere the next day, are you going to use the Post Office or Federal Express?

The total amount spent to help the stranger in the story above would come to about $120. I wonder how many tax dollars would have to be collected to result in $120 worth of help from the current government of the United States. I don't know the exact answer, but I suppose it would cost the taxpayers over $10,000 by the time it goes through various levels and committees, all with meals and transportation and staff and someone's weight and age added in. We have all heard horror stories about $1200 hammers and other outrageous things such as roads to nowhere and airports built for one congressman. If the traveling stranger was not part of a preferred group, he might not have received even a dime of government assistance.

Let's talk plain. Government forced redistribution of wealth is not justice; it is theft. Whenever government redistributes wealth, an injustice is done to both parties. People on the receiving end are put into the bondage of perpetual poverty. Government has no legal or moral authority to redistribute wealth. The only lasting solution to poverty is wealth. Government cannot create wealth. All government can do is consume wealth.

Some people think that the Bible says that money is evil. This is a false notion that originated from Satan. It is the love of money that is evil.

"For the love of money is the root of all evil: which while some coveted after, they have erred from the faith, and pierced themselves through with many sorrows" (1 Tim. 6:10).

The devil would love to see God's people in poverty. The Word tells us why Satan wants God's people, especially preachers, to be poor. He has infiltrated the church to put out a "poverty is next to godliness" doctrine. Satan especially wants preachers to have no money and drive the most beat-up car. Let's read why.

"There was a little city, and few men within it; and there came a great king against it, and besieged it, and built great bulwarks against it: Now there was found in it a poor wise man, and he by his wisdom delivered the city; yet no man remembered that same

120

poor man. Then said I, Wisdom is better than strength: nevertheless the poor man's wisdom is despised, and his words are not heard" (Eccl. 9:14-16).

Even though this wise man, through his wisdom, saved the city, no one listened to him because a poor man's words are despised. When was the last time you asked a homeless man for advice on how to prosper? Satan can't stop the preachers from preaching so he tries to make them poor, so nobody will listen. God, of course, thinks the opposite of the devil.

"Let the elders that rule well be counted worthy of double honour, especially they who labour in the word and doctrine. For the scripture saith, Thou shalt not muzzle the ox that treadeth out the corn. And, The labourer is worthy of his reward" (1 Tim. 5:17-18).

"Who goeth a warfare any time at his own charges? who planteth a vineyard, and eateth not of the fruit thereof? or who feedeth a flock, and eateth not of the milk of the flock?" (1 Cor. 9:7).

Money is neither good nor bad. Money can be used for good or evil. Giving for the sake of the gospel and to the Red Cross is good. Giving to Planned Parenthood and the Center for American Progress is evil. Social justice is evil because it stops money from going to where it will do the most good. Socialists, Marxists, progressives, and the like make an erroneous assumption that profit is immoral. It is socialism, however, that rewards laziness and failure. Not every one should get a trophy.

It may seem compassionate for government to bail out organizations to save jobs. The reality is that such an action is killing a lot more new jobs than could have been generated by letting the free enterprise system work. Which has more jobs, a production facility to make new cars or a few men working with leather to make buggy whips?

Our founding fathers set up our system of government (American free enterprise) that is consistent with the Bible in that it does not seek to give all people equal outcomes. We are all created equal and have equal opportunities for the pursuit of happiness, but we are not all expected to achieve equally. One of the best examples of this is the outcome in the life of our current president, Barack Obama. Should we all be president, or should we all just get a trophy that says we are president? We will not all achieve the same results.

"For ye have the poor with you always, and whensoever ye will ye may do them good: but me ye have not always" (Mark 14:7).

Poor is a relative term. Thanks to American Capitalism, the poor in the United States would be considered rich in most other parts of the world. However, I do admit that we need some laws so that we can truly have equal opportunities. Capitalism is not designed to be strictly a "Darwinian" survival of the fittest. In fact, our founders knew that the American free enterprise system could only be made great with moral and ethical people.

"We have no government armed with power capable of contending with human passions unbridled by morality and religion. Our Constitution was made only for a moral and religious people. It is wholly inadequate to the government of any other." John Adams

Adams and the other founders knew that we should elect godly leaders if our government is to work as it was intended. They knew the Word of God.

"Moreover thou shalt provide out of all the people able men, such as fear God, men of truth, hating covetousness; and place such over them, to be rulers of thousands, and rulers of hundreds, rulers of fifties, and rulers of tens" (Exod. 18:21).

"When the righteous are in authority, the people rejoice: but when the wicked beareth rule, the people mourn" (Prov. 29:2).

The long time work ethic in America is rooted in the Bible. There is something satisfying, fulfilling, and good about labor and productivity. That's what capitalism is all about. God has says that he will bless the work of our hands. He can't bless the work of our hands if our hands are not working.

"For even when we were with you, this we commanded you, that if any would not work, neither should he eat" (2 Thess. 3:10).

"But if any provide not for his own, and specially for those of his own house, he hath denied the faith, and is worse than an infidel" (1 Tim. 5:8).

Social justice advocates like to point out the flaws in the society of the United States. The solutions are not found in forced redistribution of wealth. That is stealing. Theft never solved anything. It is very sad to see able-bodied men relying on the government and becoming rooted deeper and deeper into perpetual poverty. They should make God their source of supply, get to work, and let God bless the work of their hands.

Government needs to get out of the way so the church can be the church by giving cheerfully and not of necessity or under compulsion. God will then bring increase. Need does not move the hand of God and begging does not move the hand of God. Only faith moves the hand of God. If need moved the hand of God, there would be no one in need, for there is an inexhaustible supply in heaven. God wants us to allow him to create wealth.

"Therefore it is of faith, that it might be by grace" (Rom. 4:16a).

"But this I say, He which soweth sparingly shall reap also sparingly; and he which soweth bountifully shall reap also bountifully. Every man according as he purposeth in his heart, so let him give; not grudgingly, or of necessity: for God loveth a cheerful giver. And God is able to make all grace abound toward you; that ye, always having all sufficiency in all things, may abound to every good work: (As it is written, He hath dispersed abroad; he hath given to the poor: his righteousness remaineth for ever. Now he that ministereth seed to the sower both minister bread for your food, and multiply your seed sown, and increase the fruits of your righteousness;) Being enriched in every thing to all bountifulness, which causeth through us thanksgiving to God" (1 Cor. 9:6-11).

"I have planted, Apollos watered; but God gave the increase" (1 Cor. 3:6).

Again, government should get out of the way and let the church be the church. Then we won't concentrate on how big a piece of the pie we have, because the pie would keep getting bigger. True social justice is not forced wealth redistribution. Biblical social justice compels each Christian to do what he can to help the "least of these."

"Jesus said unto him, Thou shalt love the Lord thy God with all thy heart, and with all thy soul, and with all thy mind. This is the first and great commandment. And the second is like unto it, Thou shalt love thy neighbour as thyself" (Matt. 22:39-40).

Government redistribution discourages cheerful giving from the heart out of love and generates resentment toward the government for taking away hard-earned money without permission. Government forced wealth transfer is not a biblical concept.

"Every man according as he purposeth in his heart, so let him give; not grudgingly, or of necessity: for God loveth a cheerful giver" (2 Cor. 9:7).

God wants to increase us all as he has invited everyone to join his family. He has made a way to do that through the giving principle of sowing and reaping. All wealth comes as a gift from God, whether you acknowledge him or not. There is no limit to his wealth, as the streets in heaven are made of pure gold. God wants to work with his people so that together they can create more and more wealth to be a blessing to the whole world as God has always desired.

"But thou shalt remember the LORD thy God: for it is he that giveth thee power to get wealth, that he may establish his covenant which he sware unto thy fathers, as it is this day" (Deut. 8:18).

"The LORD shall increase you more and more, you and your children" (Ps. 115:14).

CHAPTER TEN

SOME FINAL THOUGHTS

Let's look at Luke chapter 19 once again. The key verses that we studied were verses 24-26 where Jesus related the parable of the ten pieces of money.

"And he said unto them that stood by, Take from him the pound, and give it to him that hath ten pounds. (And they said unto him, Lord, he hath ten pounds.) For I say unto you, That unto every one which hath shall be given; and from him that hath not, even that he hath shall be taken away from him" (Luke 19:24-26).

You can almost hear the amazement in the voices of the disciples as they announced their surprise that the one who had ten pounds of increase would get the one remaining pound of the servant who buried it. If Jim Wallace, spiritual advisor to President Obama, heard Jesus say that today, I'm sure he would say, "That's not social justice." That's right, it's not. Jesus never advocated government redistribution of wealth, because stealing violates the commandments of God. In fact, forced government redistribution of wealth is an evil counterfeit of God's end-time wealth redistribution.

Government should not try to manufacture equal outcomes for people, for God does not do it. As we learned in chapter one, God offers each person salvation, but not everyone will receive it. He won't force it on people, because each of us has his or her own free will. God could force equal outcomes for us all, but that would cause everyone to suffer. When government forces equal outcomes on people, it causes everyone to suffer as well. Everyone's standard of living is diminished.

Because God has given us a free will, the only way the Lord Jesus could have forced equal outcomes for us all would be to refuse to go to the cross. If he would have failed to pay for our sins, we all would have equal outcomes. We would go to hell and be in torment for all eternity. We would all be equal, isn't that great? No, it is not. God gave us a free will and an equal opportunity to be on top with him. He would like us to all receive him and be on top, but not everyone will. His offer to be on top is not limited to preferred groups. Everyone has the equal opportunity to make it to the top with him.

"For God so loved the world, that he gave his only begotten Son, that whosoever believeth in him should not perish, but have everlasting life" (John 3:16).

"But God, who is rich in mercy, for his great love wherewith he loved us, Even when we were dead in sins, hath quickened us together with Christ, (by grace ye are saved;) And hath raised us up together, and made us sit together in heavenly places in Christ Jesus" (Eph. 2:4-6).

Capitalism is like the kingdom of God. Everyone has an opportunity to make it to the top, but there won't be equal outcomes. When government tries to manufacture equal outcomes, it brings everyone down. As people concentrate on the sizes of the pieces of the pie, the pie just keeps getting smaller. All the pieces get smaller and equal outcomes are still not achieved. This cannot be achieved as God has put into man the desire to succeed, because God wants us to succeed and prosper.

"Beloved, I wish above all things that thou mayest prosper and be in health, even as thy soul prospereth" (3 John 2).

"This book of the law shall not depart out of thy mouth; but thou shalt meditate therein day and night, that thou mayest observe to do according to all that is written therein: for then thou shalt make thy way prosperous, and then thou shalt have good success" (Jos. 1:8).

Capitalism is the most compassionate system. Capitalism is the best way to reduce poverty. It gives every man a chance to succeed, and it promotes wealth into the hands of those who serve others and have a heart to give to those less fortunate. It increases individual wealth, thus allowing individuals to give out of their increase. God has designed the needs of the poor to be met by Christians, not by the government. Government's bureaucratic shuffling of wealth accomplishes nothing.

"And though I bestow all my goods to feed the poor, and though I give my body to be burned, and have not charity [love], it profiteth me nothing" (1 Cor. 13:3).

When we please God by choosing to give out of love, it works faith, so that God rewards the giver and the giving can continue at an even a greater rate.

"Charge them that are rich in this world, that they be not highminded, nor trust in uncertain riches, but in the living God, who giveth us richly all things to enjoy; That they do good, that they be rich in good works, ready to distribute, willing to communicate; Laying up in store for themselves a good foundation against the time to come, that they may lay hold on eternal life" (1 Tim. 6:17-19).

"He that hath pity upon the poor lendeth unto the LORD; and that which he hath given will he pay him again" (Prov. 19:17).

"Give, and it shall be given unto you; good measure, pressed down, and shaken together, and running over, shall men give into your bosom. For with the same measure that ye mete withal it shall be measured to you again" Luke 6:38).

"The liberal soul shall be made fat: and he that watereth shall be watered also himself" (Prov. 11:25).

Remember, there is a big difference between being liberal with your money and being liberal with *someone else's money*. When I am liberal with my money, I am generous. When Congress is liberal with my money, they are thieves. One of the biggest problems we have in this country is that political liberals think that our money is their money to do with it as they choose. They mistakenly think we work for them but, according to our Constitution, they work for us. We should not re-elect anyone who doesn't work for the people.

Our founder's knew that for our nation to be great, our government must be based on the Bible. That's because God knew that for our country to fulfill its godly assignment to achieve greatness, it needed founders who would use the Bible as their guide. It's not a coincidence that these men came together to bring forth a new nation. Were they perfect? No, they had character flaws just like all other men. They did love God, and because they had the desire to serve God, they were used for greatness. Every person in the

Bible who did great things for God had their character flaws exposed in the Scriptures, yet God still used them. Our founders knew that our nation had to be founded by acknowledging the God of Abraham.

"Blessed is the nation whose God is the LORD: and the people whom he hath chosen for his own inheritance" (Ps. 33:12).

"Except the LORD build the house, they labour in vain that build it: except the LORD keep the city, the watchman waketh but in vain" (Ps. 127:1).

One of the more common questions I get when discussing if Jesus is a socialist is the following. What about Acts chapter 2 when the early church had all things in common?
In order to answer that question let's look at Acts 2:43-47.

"And fear came upon every soul: and many wonders and signs were done by the apostles. And all that believed were together, and had all things common; and sold their possessions and goods, and parted them to all men, as every man had need. And they, continuing daily with one accord in the temple, and breaking bread from house to house, did eat their meat with gladness and singleness of heart, Praising God, and having favour with all the people. And the Lord added to the church daily such as should be saved" (Acts 2:43-47).

Did the people of the early church in Jerusalem practice some form of communism or socialism and, if so, are we instructed to follow their example? Not knowing any details other than what we read in these verses and a few others, I suppose it may be impossible to know for sure. But it does appear that they practiced, at least for a short time, some form of communism or socialism. At the very least, they exhibited certain aspects of socialism. They shared everything in common. However, what the early church practiced was quite different from what other socialists have done throughout history.

The people of the church in Jerusalem, as described in the second chapter of the book of Acts, gave to those who had great needs. All the giving was completely voluntary. They gave freely, and there were no regulations that required them to give. Normally, socialism is carried out by the civil government. The government requires its citizens to surrender their property for the common good. Usually the collection of goods is violently enforced on those that wish to retain their property.

In real socialism, people "give" because a system of government forces them to give. They have no choice as to how much and to whom they give. The stingy man and the generous man are both required to give everything they earn. You can see no difference as to the character of each man. They all look the same, just like bricks do.

What was happening in Jerusalem that caused the early Christians to give all they had? Peter preached and 3,000 were saved. Later he preached and 5,000 were saved. This was at the time of Pentecost and Jerusalem was crowded with Jews who had come from all over the world. Many of the Jews (3,000 right off the bat) were converted to the new covenant, and most did not live in Jerusalem. Many of them wanted to linger and learn much more about their new covenant, the teachings of Christ, and how grace applied in their everyday lives before returning home. They desired more knowledge so that they could share their new faith with loved ones upon their arrival back home.

Of course, most of them hadn't planned for such a long stay. The church in Jerusalem had many new brothers in Christ who needed food and lodging immediately. In addition, this was a time of much persecution. Many new converts who lived in Jerusalem lost their jobs due to persecution and they needed help too. This was an emergency situation. With loving generosity, the people in the church brought their goods and sold what they had and laid it at the apostles' feet to distribute to those who had need.

This was not commanded. Each one made their own decision. This method of having things in common was abandoned when other people sent money to take care of the poor saints in Jerusalem. One of the men who gladly gave everything was named Joses. He sold his land and brought the money and gave it to the apostles. The apostles gave him the name Barnabus, meaning the son of consolation. He was admired by the people and became an apostle. He went on missionary journeys with Paul.

I believe that Ananias and Sapphira observed all the praise and attention that was given to Barnabus when he gave all the proceeds from the sale of his land on the island of Cyprus. I believe they decided to sell their land, hold back part of the proceeds, and give the rest to the apostles and say that they gave it all. They both fell over dead. The Bible says that they died because they lied to the Holy Ghost.

"But Peter said, Ananias, why hath Satan filled thine heart to lie to the Holy Ghost, and to keep back part of the price of the land? Whiles it remained, was it not thine own? And after it was sold, was it not in thine own power? Why hast thou conceived this thing in thine heart? Thou hast not lied unto men, but unto God" (Acts 5:3-4).

Ananias and Sapphira were not condemned for holding back some of their money. Their sin was that they lied to God. In addition, neither the civil government of Rome nor the religious government of Jewish leaders had anything to do with what happened. Peter had told Ananias that it was his land to do with what he wanted, and even after it was sold he could do what he (Ananias) wanted with the money. If Peter had mandated that they give, it would have been theft.

Let's return to a question posed earlier in this chapter. As modern day Christians, should we follow the example given by the early church in Jerusalem to have all things in common? Please be advised that not *everything* said and done in the Bible is the right thing to say and do. The great men and women revealed to us in the Scriptures often had flawed characters and acted unrighteously because of their flaws.

In fact, God seemed to go out of his way to reveal these character flaws to us in the Scriptures. I believe he did that so that we would not give up when we make mistakes. We have the example of Abraham, who is the spiritual father of us all, who told a king that Sarah was his sister. We have the example of Peter who denied Christ three times. We have the example of David, a man after God's own heart, who committed adultery with Bathsheba and had her husband killed to cover up his sin. These were examples of character flaws, not examples to follow.

All Scripture is given by inspiration of God, but not all Scripture is inspired of God. For example, Ananias and Sapphira were not inspired of God to tell a lie, but Luke, the author of the book of Acts, was inspired of God to record the truth of what they said and what they did. We should know how to rightly divide the truth, for we do not interpret Scriptures. Other Scriptures interpret Scripture.

If you interpret without benefit of other Scriptures, you will be ashamed.

"Study to shew thyself approved unto God, a workman that needeth not to be ashamed, rightly dividing the word of truth" (2 Tim. 2:15).

"Knowing this first, that no prophecy of the scripture is of any private interpretation" (2 Pet. 1:20).

The actions of Ananias and Sapphira were not given to us as an example to follow. The early church having all things in common was not an example for us to follow. There may have been some saints who were truly led by God to give all they owned. But I believe that most of the church gave under compulsion (peer pressure), or because of the great need of the new believers, when they gave everything. It wasn't taken from them; it was their decision to give it. But I believe they gave out of necessity. Not even God himself gives out of necessity.

"Every man according as he purposeth in his heart, so let him give; not grudgingly, or of necessity: for God loveth a cheerful giver" (2 Cor. 9: 7).

Obviously, there is no way to know for sure. Why do I think so? Because it didn't work. All things in common never works. Not even with sweet Christians trying to do good by giving of their own decision. There is nothing, absolutely nothing, in the Bible to support having all things in common. It goes against the primary principle of the kingdom of God, which is sowing and reaping with increase as a reward for sowing *in obedience to God.*

Having all things in common didn't work. Instead, it created great poverty like it always does. The poverty in the church at Jerusalem got worse as they were not instructed by God to live like that. If the church at Jerusalem had not abandoned this practice, they could have never fulfilled their kingdom destiny. The same holds true for any person, organization, community, or nation. The church didn't come out of poverty until the saints obeyed God and "scattered abroad throughout the regions of Judea and Samaria, except the apostles" (Acts 8:1b).

The apostle Paul took offerings for the poor church in Jerusalem. It wasn't until the new saints obeyed and began to sow their own seeds that they began to operate the way they should. The other churches became blessed as they gave.

"But now I go unto Jerusalem to minister unto the saints. For it hath pleased them of Macedonia and Achaia to make a certain contribution for the poor saints which are at Jerusalem" (Rom. 15:25-26).

"Now concerning the collection for the saints, as I have given order to the churches of Galatia, even so do ye. Upon the first day of the week let every one of you lay by him in store, as God hath prospered him, that there be no gatherings when I come. And when I come, whomsoever ye shall approve by your letters, them will I send to bring your liberality unto Jerusalem" (1 Cor. 16:1-3).

The members of the Jerusalem church saw a need, and out of love, they tried to do right but they were wrong. They should not be our example. You can do the right thing the wrong way. They may have even placed themselves under a curse for operating in this evil system. Why else would Ananias and Sapphira fall over dead?

Perhaps they made a vow to God and did not do their part. We really don't know.

The church of Jerusalem tried to do the right thing, but they did it the wrong way. Here's an example of someone doing the right thing the wrong way, not according to the Scriptures. Remember when David wanted to bring the Ark of the Covenant to Zion.

"Again, David gathered together all the chosen men of Israel, thirty thousand. And David arose, and went with all the people that were with him from Baale of Judah, to bring up from thence the ark of God, whose name is called by the name of the LORD of hosts that dwelleth between the cherubims. And they set the ark of God upon a new cart, and brought it out of the house of Abinadab that was in Gibeah: and Uzzah and Ahio, the sons of Abinadab, drave the new cart. And they brought it out of the house of Abinadab which was at Gibeah, accompanying the ark of God: and Ahio went before the ark. And David and all the house of Israel played before the LORD on all manner of instruments made of fir wood, even on harps, and on psalteries, and on timbrels, and on cornets, and on cymbals. And when they came to Nachon's threshingfloor, Uzzah put forth his hand to the ark of God, and took hold of it; for the oxen shook it. And the anger of the LORD was kindled against Uzzah; and God smote him there for his error; and there he died by the ark of God" (2 Sam. 1:1-7).

David was doing the right thing the wrong way, and it brought a curse and somebody fell over dead. Sound familiar? As the new king, David had a right to bring the Ark to his hometown. There was no problem in moving the Ark, but it was not moved the right way according to the Scriptures. He had placed the Ark on a cart drawn by two oxen. He was not careful to follow God's instructions for carrying the Ark.

"And Moses took the wagons and the oxen, and gave them unto the Levites. Two wagons and four oxen he gave unto the sons of Gershon, according to their service: And four wagons and eight oxen he gave unto the sons of Merari, according unto their service, under the hand of Ithamar the son of Aaron the priests. But unto the sons of Kohath he gave none: because the service of the sanctuary belonging unto them was that they should bear upon their shoulders" (Num. 7:6-9).

David's disobedience caused a death and stopped God's prosperity towards Jerusalem. When David did it right according to the Scriptures, prosperity resumed. David checked the Scriptures, found his problem, and then did the right thing the right way, according to the Scriptures, and the people were blessed.

"And David called for Zadok and Abiathar the priests, and for the Levites, for Uriel, Asaiah, and Joel, Shemaiah, and Eliel, and Amminadab, And said unto them, Ye are the chief of the fathers of the Levites: sanctify yourselves, both ye and your brethren, that ye may bring up the ark of the LORD God of Israel unto the place that I have prepared for it. For because ye did it not at the first, the LORD our God made a breach upon us, for that we sought him not after the due order. So the priests and the Levites sanctified themselves to bring up the ark of the LORD God of Israel. And the children of the Levites bare the ark of God upon their shoulders with the staves thereon, as Moses commanded according to the word of the LORD" (1 Chron. 15:11-15).

The early church in Jerusalem made some mistakes. With no one left with resources, the entire church became poor—needing help instead of being able to continue to give. God's way always enables the giver to receive increase to be able to give even more. Once they changed their ways and received some help, they started to prosper. Having all things in common never works and is never scriptural. If God has called you personally to sell all things and give it all, then that is fine for you. That is not his call on everyone. His call for everyone is to make Jesus your top priority and stand ready to give whatever and however you are lead by the Holy Ghost.

Another frequently asked question that challenges the notion that U. S. Constitution was ordained of God is the following. Why did the constitution allow slavery?

In reality, it did not allow slavery. Coupled with the Declaration of Independence and the Bill of Rights, the U.S. Constitution is the reason that slavery could not last in the United States of America. Frederick Douglass agreed with me even before slavery was abolished. Below is a quote from his speech on the Dred Scott decision. He said it better than I ever could.

> "I base my sense of the certain overthrow of slavery, in part, upon the nature of the American Government, the Constitution, the tendencies of the age, and the character of the American people; and this, notwithstanding the important decision of Judge Taney. I know of no soil better adapted to the growth of reform than American soil. I know of no country where the conditions for affecting great changes in the settled order of things, for the development of right ideas of liberty and humanity, are more favorable than here in these United States. The very groundwork of this government is a good repository of Christian civilization. The Constitution, as well as the Declaration of Independence, and the sentiments of the founders of

the Republic, give us a plat-form broad enough, and strong enough, to support the most comprehensive plans for the freedom and elevation of all the people of this country, without regard to color, class, or clime....When I admit that slavery is constitutional, I must see slavery recognized in the Constitution. I must see that it is there plainly stated that one man of a certain description has a right of property in the body and soul of another man of a certain description. There must be no room for a doubt. In a matter so important as the loss of liberty, everything must be proved beyond all reasonable doubt. The well known rules of legal interpretation bear me out in this stub-born refusal to see slavery where slavery is not.... Now let us approach the Constitution from the standpoint thus indicated, and instead of finding in it a warrant for the stupendous system of robbery, comprehended in the term slavery, we shall find it strongly against that system....Neither in the preamble nor in the body of the Constitution is there a single mention of the term slave or slave holder, slave master or slave state, neither is there any reference to the color, or the physical peculiarities of any part of the people of the United States. Neither is there anything in the Constitution standing alone, which would imply the existence of slavery in this country....I ask, then, any man to read the Constitution, and tell me where, if he can, in what particular that instrument affords the slightest sanction of slavery? Where will he find a guarantee for slavery? Will he find it in the declaration that no person shall be deprived of life, liberty, or property, without due process of law?

Will he find it in the declaration that the Constitution was established to secure the blessing of liberty? Will he find it in the right of the people to be secure in their persons and papers, and houses, and effects? Will he find it in the clause prohibiting the enactment by any State of a bill of attainder? These all strike at the root of slavery, and any one of them, but faith-fully carried out, would put an end to slavery in every State in the American Union....Thus the very essence of the whole slave code is in open violation of a fundamental provision of the Constitution, and is in open and flagrant violation of all the objects set forth in the Constitution....The answer is ready. The Constitution is one thing, its administration is another, and, in this instance, a very different and opposite thing. I am here to vindicate the law, not the administration of the law. It is the written Constitution, not the unwritten Constitution, that is now before us. If, in the whole range of the Constitution, you can find no warrant for slavery, then we may properly claim it for liberty."

It is requisite to be reminded that our founders were men who had flaws. In spite of that, they followed the leading of the Spirit of God to give us the greatest model of civil government that has ever existed on earth. It was born of God to coincide with the heart of God and the laws of God to bless our nation, so that through us all the nations of the world might be blessed.

There is currently a demonic attack to denounce, reprove, undermine, collapse, and utterly destroy the United States of America. It is a unified effort of ungodly forces just as destructive as was the building of the Tower of Babel. This coalition of evil contains such groups as progressives, socialists, communists, social justice activists, Marxists, union leaders, those touting liberation theology, and Muslim extremists.

Those of us who believe in Jesus, who believe that God loves Israel, who believe in the greatness of our founding documents, and are proud of this nation's godly heritage, need to stand against this evil force. We must do it God's way. We practice our civil responsibilities, we pray for our leaders and for our nation, and we stand up and speak the truth in love. We do not hate people who have gone astray; we just hate their ideas. We should love the people and lead them to Jesus, but we cannot compromise. God's way is always the best way.

"For we wrestle not against flesh and blood, but against principalities, against powers, against the rulers of the darkness of this world, against spiritual wickedness in high places" (Eph. 6:12).

"Recompense to no man evil for evil. Provide things honest in the sight of all men. If it be possible, as much as lieth in you, live peaceably with all men. Dearly beloved, avenge not yourselves, but rather give place unto wrath: for it is written, Vengeance is mine; I will repay, saith the Lord. Therefore if thine enemy hunger, feed him; if he thirst, give him drink: for in so doing thou shalt heap coals of fire on his head. Be not overcome of evil, but overcome evil with good" (Rom. 12:17-21).

If we fail to recognize what is happening and ignore what the devil is doing, we will have to answer to God. We can no longer depend on the ungodly to do right. We must do right. Our nation's destiny is still in the hands of God's people.

"If my people, which are called by my name, shall humble themselves, and pray, and seek my face, and turn from their wicked ways; then will I hear from heaven, and will forgive their sin, and will heal their land" (2 Chron. 7:14).

You and I can make the difference! Freedom was given to us from God and we must not let go of it at any cost. Any elected official who takes an oath to defend and protect the Constitution and then fails to do so should not be given another term in office by the voters. If we stick our heads in the sand, we will regret it.

This sentiment is captured perfectly in the following quote from Ronald Reagan, one of our greatest presidents.

"Freedom is never more than one generation away from extinction. We didn't pass it to our children in the bloodstream. It must be fought for, protected, and handed on for them to do the same, or one day we will spend our sunset years telling our children what it was once like in the United States where men were free."[1]

"Government exists to protect us from each other. Where government has gone beyond its limits is in deciding to protect us from ourselves."[2] Ronald Reagan

Endnotes

Chapter 1:

End-Time Harvest

> [1]Sutton, Hilton, *The Book of Revelation Revealed,* (New Caney, Texas: Hilton Sutton World Ministries, 2006), p. 79
>
> [2]Sutton, H. ibid, p.80
>
> [3]Sutton, H. ibid
>
> [4]Sutton, H. ibid, p. 81

Chapter 8:

One Nation Under God

> [1]Sutton, Hilton, *As the United States Goes, So Goes the World,* (New Caney,
> Texas: Hilton Sutton World Ministries) p. 29
>
> [2]Isi Leibler, *The Case For Israel*, (Australia, The Globe Press, 1972), p. 15
>
> [3]jewishvirtuallibrary.org/jsource/History/1948_War.html

[4]Sutton, Hilton, *As the United States Goes, So Goes the World,* (New Caney Texas: Hilton Sutton World Ministries) p. 5

[5]Origins of American Constitution, 1987

[6]Sutton, Hilton, *As the United States Goes, So Goes the World,* (New Caney, Texas: Hilton Sutton World Ministries) p. 69

Chapter 9:

Capitalism, Socialism, Marxism, and Social Justice

[1]http://www.aipnews.com/talk/forums/thread-view.asp?tid=187

Chapter 10:

Some Final Thoughts

[1]http://www.brainyquote.com/quotes/authors/r/ronald_reagan.html

[2]http://www.brainyquote.com/quotes/authors/r/ronald_reagan.html

RECOMMENDED READINGS

As the U.S. Goes, So Goes the World by Hilton Sutton

How to Function in This Economy by Gerald W. Davis

America's Godly Heritage by David Barton

The Book of Revelation Revealed by Hilton Sutton

Inhabiting Eternity on Earth by David Hope

What others are saying ......

"Pastor David shares deep insight with us as he delves into questions that many have skipped over in the Bible. He boldly attacks issues such as: Is money is evil? How do we receive security for tomorrow? Was Jesus being fair when he taught about the talents? All this and more in this book *Jesus of Nazareth, Socialist or Capitalist?* Good job Pastor Hope!

Pastor Roger DeWitt
Spring, TX

"This compelling work by Christian Author David Hope aroused my passions. I found it inspirational, thought provoking and penned by a true patriot and lover of liberty! Inspirational because it was packed full of encouragement to be all that we were created to be, to rise up and lay hold of our God given destinies, and to realize that Christians have all been endowed with gifts from above and given the great opportunity to be participants in the End Time Harvest of Souls. Thought provoking because Reverend Hope clears away the confusion by wielding forth the sword of truth. I love his no nonsense one liners chocked full of biblical principles and practical application. In *Jesus of Nazareth, Socialist or Capitalist?,* the author draws a line in the sand and states his case against forced government redistribution of wealth and proclaims that the best days of the glorious and triumphant Church of the Lord Jesus Christ lie ahead."

Lee Short, Missionary to Mexico/Founder and President of Vida International

Dear Pastor David, I just finished reading your book titled *Jesus of Nazareth, Socialist or Capitalist?* I so deeply appreciate your effort in the writing of this book. I found it to be so timely and so well structured. You obviously did your homework on its contents. I am in100% agreement with your position taken here. I only hope that every pastor will have an opportunity to read it. There is so much departure from the absolutes and the true intent of the scripture. So many preachers are modifying and compromising the message of the Bible from the pulpit today. Political correctness has taken its toll on the purity and the intent of the written Word. It is time for the church to stand up and speak up. I applaud you for this work and pray indeed that it will be a best seller.

Your friend and fellow worker,
Gerald Davis, D.D.
Overflowing Cup Ministries

Other books from David Hope

Inhabiting Eternity on Earth

God's Perspective on Money

Do You Want to be Healed?

The Goodness of God

Other Books from RevMedia Publishing

Almost Out of Grace by David Yanez

Military Life and the Power of God by David Yanez

How to Function in this Economy by Gerald Davis

Wee Boys from Glasgow Don't Cry by Peter Stanway

Out of the Snare by Lois Thomson-Bowersock

To order more books of Jesus of Nazareth, Socialist or Capitalist? or any other of the books on this page. Please visit our website www.revmediapublishing.com

You can also visit your local bookstore or online book merchant

Prayer for Salvation

Life is not as complicated as most people think. If you are in covenant with Jesus, all you have to do is please him and everything else takes care of itself. Trust in God and make him your source of supply and by faith you can live on earth like it is in heaven.

"Therefore take no thought, saying, What shall we eat? Or, Wherewithal shall we be clothed? (for after all these things do the Gentiles seek) for your heavenly Father knowth that ye have need of all these things. But seek ye first the Kingdom of God and his righteousness; and all these things shall be added unto you."(Mt 6:31-33)

Those that have entered into a blood covenant with God by being born again by the spirit of God have eternal life and can walk in health and prosper.

"Beloved, I wish above all things that thou mayest proper and be in health, even as thy soul prospereth."(3Jn2)

Remember, God does not automatically heal and prosper you. We have to call upon his promises in the name of Jesus. Every good thing comes to us through Jesus. The only qualification to receive from the Father is that we know his Jesus. We have to have made Jesus our Lord and Savior.

Every one needs Jesus because our sins have separated us from a holy God. There is not anyone who has not told a lie or committed a sin. God, however, is holy and cannot fellowship with sin.

So he sent his son, Jesus, to be a man and pay for our sins that we might have the righteousness of God.

Jesus took on our sins and by faith we can receive the exchange of his righteousness and therefore boldly enter into the throne of grace. It's not based on what we have done but what Jesus has done for us. If you will receive Jesus, you will never have to be ashamed again, for Jesus will not be ashamed of you.

"For both he that sanctifieth and they who are sanctified are all of one: for which cause he is not ashamed to call them brethren."(He 2:11)

Because of the sin of Adam, we stand condemned until we receive Jesus by faith. Jesus did not come into the world to condemn the world but to set us free from the condemnation we are already in. It is a free gift of God. We simply receive it by faith.

"Therefore as by the offence of the judgement came upon all men to condemnation: even so by the righteousness of one free gift upon all men unto justification of life. For as by one man's disobedience many were made sinners, so by the obedience of one shall many be made righteous. More over the law entered, that the offence might abound. But where sin abounded, grace did much more abound: That as sin hath reigned unto death, even so might grace reign through righteousness unto eternal life by Jesus Christ our Lord."(Ro 5:18-21)

If you have never received Jesus into your heart but you would like to, then pray this prayer and mean it in your heart. You will inherit eternal life and can begin walking in your inheritance by receiving provision and health on this earth in the name of Jesus.

Lord Jesus, I am a sinner. Forgive me of my sins, come into my heart and make me brand new. Wash me clean in your precious blood. I confess you as my Lord and Savior and I will serve you all the days of my life. Jesus, thank you for saving me and I thank you that I am now a child of God and my name is written in Heaven. I thank you that I now can call upon your name for healing and provision. Help me to make you my source of supply for every area of my life.   AMEN

Prayer for Healing

Jesus wants you healed. All we have to do is ask and believe his word.

"And Jesus departed from thence, and came nigh unto the Sea of Galilee; and went up into a mountain, and sat down there. And great multitudes came unto him, having with them those that were lame, blind, dumb, and many others, and cast them down at Jesus' feet; and he healed them: insomuch that the multitude wondered, when they saw the dumb to speak, the maimed to be whole, the lame to walk, and the blind to see: and they glorified the God of Israel."(Mt 15:29-31)

You see, it's the healing that glorifies God, sickness only glorifies the devil. You can still glorify God when you are sick but God is never glorified in sickness. Great multitudes came to Jesus and he healed them all. To me a multitude of people is as many people as the eye can see. A great multitude of people is more than that. Great multitudes are even more than that. Yet Jesus did not turn even one person away but healed them all.

Some people think that God won't heal them because of some bad things they have done. Healing is for whosoever will receive it by faith. It is not based on performance. Don't you think that in great multitudes that there is at least one person whose performance is worse than yours? Yet, Jesus healed them.

In great multitudes you will find every kind of person. You'll find rich and poor, young and old, and every ethnic background. In great multitudes, there are educated people and those with no schooling, people from good families and people from bad families. There are those that are married, singled and divorced. There are people with religious training and people who have never even prayed before. There are kind people and mean people. There are people who are sexually pure and those that have performed perversion. There are all kinds of people. Jesus healed them all.

God desires greatly for us to receive our healing. Jesus took 39 stripes on his back so that we could be healed. Jesus will never say no to your healing. If Jesus wanted to say no, he wouldn't have had to take one stripe. He didn't take stripes on his back to say no, he took the stripes so that he could say, YES! Pray this prayer out loud and believe God for healing.

Father,

I come to you in the name of Jesus. I give you thanks that by your stripes I was healed and I receive it now by faith. I speak God life and resurrection power into my body to make me whole from the top of my head to the soles of my feet for the glory of God. I release my faith for it and count it as already done in the name of Jesus. Amen.

Please visit us at Words of Life Church....

David Hope is the Senior Pastor of Words of Life Church, a non-denominational, spirit filled, family church located in Humble, Texas. If you're in the Houston/Humble area please join us for service.

Words of Life Church
7811 FM 1960
Humble TX 77346

Service Times:
Sunday Morning 10:40am
Sunday Evening 6:00pm
Wednesday Evening 7:00pm

www.wordsoflifechurch.net

Notes

Notes

Notes

Notes

Notes

www.ingramcontent.com/pod-product-compliance
Lightning Source LLC
LaVergne TN
LVHW051100080426
835508LV00019B/1993